TRAUMATIC RELIVING IN HISTORY, LITERATURE, AND FILM

TRAUMATIC RELIVING IN HISTORY, LITERATURE, AND FILM

Rudolph Binion

KARNAC

First published in 2011 by
Karnac Books Ltd
118 Finchley Road
London NW3 5HT

British Library Cataloguing in Publication Data

A C.I.P. for this book is available from the British Library

ISBN-13: 978-1-85575-743-1

Typeset by Vikatan Publishing Solutions (P) Ltd., Chennai, India

www.karnacbooks.com

For Eléna

Beyond the compass of a wife
She verges on an edge of life
Where species mingle, beasts don't bite,
And donkeys dine by candlelight.

"All miserable events do naturally beget their like."

—Herman Melville, *Moby-Dick*

"I had the feeling as in a nightmare of its all being something repeated, something I had been through and that now I must go through again."

—Ernest Hemingway, *The Sun Also Rises*

CONTENTS

FOREWORD

This book is about a rare but highly significant psychological mechanism that has yet to be seen for what it is. By a "psychological mechanism" I mean a set course of human behaviour such that, once it kicks in, there is no stopping it. The one to be discussed has often been observed at work in everyday life, although without being recognized as the distinct mechanism that it is. Psychologists in particular have overlooked its patterned workings, which they lump together with others or else parcel out under various distinct rubrics. I propose to track and trace those workings through history, literature, and film with the aim of defining their specificity. Creative writers since antiquity and especially film-makers in our own times have drawn on this mechanism to dramatic and even comic effect with at least an intuitive grasp of its independent reality and uncanny force. But history is the prime showcase for its incidence on individual and mass behaviour alike. It intrudes on history only exceptionally, but when it does it sweeps all before it.

What is this mechanism? All too simply put, it is the occasional felt need to repeat, to re-enact, to relive an unbearable experience. But this formulation is obviously deficient: who would want to re-experience something unbearable? What needs adding is that the repetition is unconscious. The unbearable experience is re-run without being recognized. It looks different, but it feels the same deep down. And it feels the same because it is the same in disguise. Not every unbearable experience is repeated, however, even in disguise—far from it. Who, then, repeats which unbearable experiences, and why? This is the complex question behind all the words ahead.

Such repetition can be divined behind one news item after another. A woman committed for crying "Fire!" in the basement of a department store turns out to have survived, and almost forgotten, a devastating nightclub fire long years before. A seemingly readjusted Vietnam veteran is arrested in a cemetery shouting orders to a nonexistent platoon to attack a nearby police station. A child molester, when interrogated, claims to have suffered in the act, then remembers that he himself had been painfully raped as a child: a classic role reversal. A stretch of coast line that is periodically wiped out by floods is each time resettled by the survivors once they find false closure. The pattern is discernible at a glance. I propose to try to define it exactly and then to look behind it.

The short word for such an unbearable experience that may get recycled is "trauma". As a rule, people who suffer a traumatic experience do not find closure easily—which is just as well, for the price of their putting the experience behind them, as the expression goes, is that they may then contrive to repeat it unknowingly at a later point. We do not puzzle over the compulsive, vivid remembering of a trauma, however painful and pointless, because that is the familiar, normal reaction. For the opposite reason we do not puzzle over repeating a trauma unawares: because the process has not been properly discerned even though it is instinctively known to us all and often evident at a glance. Again, the aim of this book is to make that evidence precise and that knowledge explicit.

My concern is, then, with the human peculiarity of occasionally contriving to repeat a traumatic experience in a disguise thick enough to fool the traumatized subject but thin enough for an outside observer to see through, especially since Freud alerted the world to the common forms that unconscious disguises take. Simple opposites, such as carnal for chaste or tutor for tutee, are about as thick as such disguises ever get. I draw these two tiny, tidy examples from the first case of traumatic reliving that I encountered in my historic researches, Lou Andreas-Salomé's routinized rehash in life and letters of her traumatic break-up with Friedrich Nietzsche. Ever since this first encounter with traumatic reliving in history I have been prone to hit up against it repeatedly whether on the individual or the group level—or even both at once, as with Hitler and his following reliving separate traumas in sync. My own repetitive pattern was not, then, itself trauma-induced—or did Lou's trauma set it going? Once I thought to escape it by way of a book on literary classics, only to come upon it again and again in fiction since antiquity. And most recently, after I complained to my wife about my recurrent encounters with recurrent trauma, she found herself spotting it in one movie after another. So I finally resolved to consolidate my findings on traumatic reliving in fact and fancy—for the prospective benefit of learning, to be sure, but also in hopes of finally kicking the curse.

My wife, Eléna Lagrange, encouraged and assisted me in this endeavour well beyond the film research, at which she beat me cold. Alice Binion and Deborah Hayden each gave me invaluable feedback along my way. Philippe d'Hugues provided me with several precious leads on film. Stephen Kern annotated the whole manuscript incisively, and Barry Shapiro gave a near-final draft a sharp critical overview. To all, my apologies for rewarding their generous support so poorly in that my findings raise more problems than they even begin to solve. At least those problems are now raised.

ABOUT THE AUTHOR

Born on 18 January 1927 in New York, Rudolph Binion was educated at Columbia University and the University of Paris. He served two years in the United States Army and worked three years in demographic statistics at UNESCO (Paris) before taking a doctorate in History at Columbia in 1958. By then he had begun teaching—one year in intellectual history at Rutgers University, three years in the humanities at MIT, and eight years in intellectual history at Columbia. In 1967 he moved to Brandeis University, where he has remained ever since except for a visiting professorship at the Collège de France (Paris) in 1980. He has published ten books and some fifty scholarly articles in European and American political, social, and demographic history, biography, art, and literature. But ever since his monumental psychobiography of the prodigious Russo-German woman of letters Lou Andreas-Salomé, *Frau Lou* (1968), his constant preoccupation in all of his research has been with developing psychohistorical method, and this increasingly with a focus on "group process", or human groups acting in concert without their members' awareness. In his numerous individual and, more recently, group studies he has repeatedly found himself dealing with the unconscious repetition of traumatic experiences. In his present book he draws on his life's work with "traumatic reliving" in history, and adds comparative studies of the same phenomenon in literature and film, in an attempt to define the process of traumatic reliving by individuals and groups and to understand who relives which traumas why.

CHAPTER ONE

Reliving

Reliving is live repetition. Repetition is the way of the material world—set courses of change, regular runs and re-runs, self-identical cycles and sequences, reprises unending. Life, having been born of the material world, does not escape this rule of recurrence. Before it comes full circle in death, living is mostly reliving, even short of the eternal return hypothesized by a latter-day seer, or of being trapped in a closed loop of time like tempunauts in science fiction.[1] Animals, although self-propelled, feel and act repetitively by instinct, reflex, and habit. Groups of animals likewise survive by routine, as in seasonal migrations. And humans, themselves "repetition machines",[2] contribute often senseless personal patterns of behaviour to the replicative repertoire of the natural world. To be sure, not all conduct, animal or especially human, is repetitive, in confirmation whereof I tried horseradish once and never tried it again. Yet repetition, insidious repetition, is the rule with animate as with inanimate matter, however uncertain its next moment may often be.

---

[1] Nietzsche (1887): IV: 341; Dick (1974).
[2] Janet (1928): 211.

Among the living, repetition comes in numerous variants. Before repeating its own acts, an animal will mostly repeat other animals' acts, at least until they become its own. When animals repeat their own acts, they relive them. With humans specifically, memory intensifies physical reliving and, further, enables imaginary reliving—the recall of bygone sensations together with the feelings they aroused. Such recall may come about spontaneously within a closed-off stream of consciousness. Or it may be touched off from the outside, as when the distinctive taste of a piece of pastry dipped in herbal tea famously triggered seven fictional volumes about recovering the past.[3] That taste was a pleasant one, so its original, which it brought back to mind, was as welcome a recall as the stuff of most rumination. Joys like to be remembered, even memorialized. By contrast, a chance reminder of a painful experience will sooner evoke a wince than release a flood of recollections.

A wince is a feeble, failed denial. Any sudden painful recall, however occasioned, will invite at least that much would-be denial, however fleeting. Indeed, a painful experience will itself already invite denial, however fleeting—denial that it is happening or has happened, and afterwards denial that it mattered as, however, those very denials show that it did. One way of denying that a painful experience mattered is to construe it as just one more in a familiar series of like occurrences. If, against all the odds, a painful experience is successfully denied, a chance reminder of it will elicit an eerie déjà vu. Normally, however, a painful experience cannot itself be denied; rather, the pain alone, detached from the sensory memory, will be blocked or filtered out at the source. By the pain of an overly painful experience I mean here and hereafter the mental pain: physical pain does not behave the same way. And by mental pain I mean the intense affect, whatever it may be—shame, horror, fear, anguish, distress—that made and makes the experience unbearable.

Above a certain threshold of pain, the scenario broadens and deepens in scope. With failed denial comes would-be undoing—the futile impulse to cancel an overly painful experience as if magically or to prevent it after the fact. Once that brief impulse passes, such an overly painful experience, or trauma, will as a rule be recalled incessantly,

[3] Proust (1913–1927).

waking or sleeping, with the original affect reviving along with it. The experience may, however, be largely screened or blurred in the recall in order to mitigate the attendant pain even while remaining potentially accessible intact and in full.

A therapy developed especially since the late 1980s for overwhelming trauma aims to induce total, straight recall of the traumatic experience, affect inclusive, as if the wound could heal by being ripped wide open again. Fiction having the jump on fact, such so-called reliving therapy[4] was already imagined once by the novelist Honoré de Balzac and again by the playwright Luigi Pirandello. In Balzac's story, as in Pirandello's play, the traumatic event was even replicated for therapeutic purposes, with duly disastrous results. The heroine of Balzac's "Adieu" of 1830 goes mad when she must leave her officer lover to his fate in the bloody retreat of Napoleon's army from Moscow; he survives to re-stage their battlefield adieu for her with her doctor's help in a shock therapy that at once both cures and kills her.[5] And in Pirandello's *Henry IV* of 1922, a psychiatrist re-stages around the hero the masquerade party at which a villain pricked his horse, which then threw him traumatically; instead of curing him, however, the re-staging prompts a traumatic turnabout whereby the hero runs the villain through. (He had meanwhile recovered in secret not from the trauma itself, but from its initial shock effect: the delusion that he really was the emperor Henry IV, as whom he was masquerading).[6]

Induced reliving as in Balzac, Pirandello, or some psychiatric practice is emphatically not to be confused with the spontaneous, unsuspecting reliving of a traumatic experience in fact or fancy beneath a surface disguise. Such spontaneous, unsuspecting reliving can be either chronic or episodic—either a steady symptom expressing the trauma symbolically or a discrete performance recapitulating it symbolically. The latter, the episodic reliving of a traumatic experience in all its crucial particulars, has drawn little scientific notice.[7]

---

[4]More recently called "exposure therapy" or "narrative exposure therapy", it was foreshadowed in clinical practice by Pierre Janet with an admixture of hypnotherapy.

[5]Balzac (1834–1850/1979).

[6]Pirandello (1922/1947).

[7]The phenomenon has occasionally been glimpsed without being sorted out, perhaps most closely in Van der Kolk (1987) and Van der Kolk (1989); Terr (1990): 261–280 and passim; Chu (1991): 327–332; Caruth (1996); Levy (2000): 45–53; and Orlandini (2004).

Even Freud, who initially construed all neuroses as chronic traumatic relivings, afterwards constructed for them a theoretical framework recalcitrant to traumatic reliving of whichever kind, chronic or episodic: his paradoxical contribution will be discussed in Chapter 1. Meanwhile it needs heavy stressing here at the outset that not all repetitive behaviour is trauma-driven, any more than all trauma gets relived. Most repetition is merely inertial; most shocks are simply absorbed. As for bursts of joy that overwhelm like traumas, they are not, like traumas, put out of mind insofar as they can be, and for that reason alone are not in line to be relived unsuspectingly—which is just as well, for even symbolically it would be no cinch to replicate a windfall unawares.

Some prolegomena (irresistible mouthful!) to this enquiry are overdue. Human conduct is mostly actuated from within, and then mostly unconsciously: whoever sees it differently may as well quit right here. Traumatic reliving by individuals is unconscious all the way; that is, those individuals who relive a trauma are never aware of reliving it even if they do remember it in the process. Groups relive as do individuals, if perhaps somewhat more primitively on balance, with the peculiar twist that one or another member of a group may see and feel when the group as a whole is reliving. And the common mode of reliving by groups and individuals, which will be explored, has not changed since antiquity as far as I can tell.

Because it involves unconscious recall and rehash, traumatic reliving can have begun only with the human breed—unless, as in the Greek *Theogony*, it began with the gods and passed among them from father to son. There the earth, namely Gaia, emerged from chaos and bore the sky, alias Uranus, to cover her. Lusty Uranus impregnated mother Gaia relentlessly, breeding three races of giants including the titans and burying them all alive in her earthy folds. Womb-weary at last, Gaia induced one of her titanic sons, Cronus, to lop off the paternal member at its next eager approach. Through this gory, gooey deed the sky devolved on Cronus, who promptly set about inseminating his sister Rhea without a let-up, only to swallow each new offspring fresh upon delivery lest one supplant him in his turn. Rhea, however, tricked him into swallowing a swaddled stone in lieu of newborn Zeus, whom she hid in Crete with Gaia's connivance. Zeus grew up to usurp the sky with the help of his wise and wily spouse, Metis: she fed his brutish father an emetic such that he regurgitated the swaddled stone followed by the whole brood of Zeus's undigested elder siblings. Afterwards ingrate Zeus swallowed pregnant Metis in one godly gulp when Gaia warned him that a daughter by Metis could outwit him or a son dethrone him. In due course Athena sprang full-blown from his head while Metis remained intact beneath his vitals, her sharp wits enabling him to rule the sky ever after. In the final tally, Cronus had relived his traumatic dethronement of Uranus, Gaia aiding, with the child-burying converted into child-swallowing, whereupon Zeus had relived Cronus's traumatic reliving, with the child-swallowing recast as wife-swallowing. Only later did the titan Prometheus create mankind.

A staple of old legend, ancestral trauma relived has haunted new legend as well. Thus in Franz Grillparzer's *The Ancestress* of 1817, a Romantic so-called "tragedy of fate", the traumatic precedent set by an adulteress, murdered in sin like Dante's Francesca, haunts her posterity through periodic domestic disasters until her line expires climactically in parricide and incest. Traumas of the dead commonly haunt the living in ghost stories; a classic cinematic instance is Richard Loncraine's *Full Circle* (also called *The Haunting of Julia*) of 1977. And as in creative fantasy, so in real life, one can relive not just a trauma of one's own, but another's trauma (usually an older blood relative's) as if it were one's own. This is puzzling, even baffling. Even more baffling is that groups as such can suffer and relive traumas about like individuals. In fact groups often acquire, and always firm up, their collective identities as a result of traumas suffered together and then relived in concert. Such reliving by groups implies group memory both conscious and unconscious—an inconceivable, but inescapable, implication. The group function looks like a vestige of our long history as hunter-gatherers operating in widely dispersed bands, the way Euripides' regressive bacchae, although dispersed on Mount Cithaeron, would bound about "as though with a single mind";[8] still, vestige or no, the physiology of that "single mind" eludes detection. Hardly less puzzling, finally, is why an individual or a group should keep on painfully remembering a painful trauma, let alone relive it instead, and then with a fury—or indeed keep reliving it, as on an unmerry-go-round. "That was no

---

[8]Euripides (406 B.C.): 44, line 692.

fun, so here goes again!" looks like nothing so much as a misprint. I propose to try at least to illuminate, if not to solve, these human mysteries through a comparative look at several specific historic cases of traumatic reliving supplemented by fictional and cinematic examples that have enjoyed unquestioning public acceptance as true-to-life. I hope thereby to shed needful new light not just on traumatic reliving itself, but also on its two components—trauma and reliving—separately.

The vast corpus of recent trauma studies is mostly off my subject. Not only do trauma theorists tend to ignore episodic traumatic reliving, or at least miss its specificity; they lean too hard on the diagnostic category of "post-traumatic stress disorder" established by the American Psychiatric Association in the early 1980s, which standardized the definition of psychological trauma as drastic physical shock followed by persistent anxious recall or else, on the contrary, by memory blockage. Historic case studies show, however, that purely emotional as well as physical shock may entail episodic reliving, and without either stressful recall or memory blockage. On the other hand, clinical studies of post-traumatic stress can elucidate historic behaviour that reflects such stress in individuals alone or within groups as such,[9] but that is not my subject.

Many of the fundamentals stated in this introduction will be echoed and re-echoed below for clarity's sake. May such redundancy offend less in a book about reliving.

---

[9]See, for example, Shapiro (2009) on how anxiety and denial influenced the work of the French Constituent Assembly after its traumatically felt threat of June–July 1789 from the nearly thirty thousand royal troops surrounding it.

CHAPTER TWO

Reliving with Freud

Contriving unknowingly to repeat an especially painful experience in disguise, and more than once as circumstances permit, is a pattern of human behaviour sufficiently distinct to deserve a technical name: episodic traumatic reliving. Sigmund Freud opened the way to understanding this bizarre phenomenon even though he never dealt with it clinically or even recognized it as an entity unto itself. He did see his early neurotic patients as continually reliving traumatic experiences—sometimes fresh, more often stale—but in a static form: condensed, compounded, and converted into stable symptoms. His early constructions on such symptomatic reliving, though they were in continual flux, are known collectively as his "traumatic theory of neurosis", which was the forerunner of psychoanalysis proper. Psychoanalysis proper is commonly dated from Freud's abandonment, by the end of 1897, of his sudden, ephemeral, ill-conceived notion that all neurosis originates in early sexual abuse and his recognition that such abuse is commonly fantasized by the child. It can be dated more consequently, if still less precisely, from Freud's assumption, developed gradually thereafter in the late 1890s, that every adult neurosis derives from an infantile original whatever later disturbances it may reflect as well. On going psychoanalytical, Freud did not relinquish the idea that neurotics are all reliving distilled traumatic material, far from it, so long as the term "traumatic" is taken to cover upsets, fixations, conflicts, and forbidden impulses indifferently, as in his own loose initial usage; not until well into World War I did he settle on the strict and narrow sense of trauma as an unmanageably shattering experience of a kind with shell shock.[1] It bears restating and emphasizing for clarity's sake that from first to last the neurotics within Freud's purview were all reliving their traumatic material of the sort chronically, in the form of fixed, steady symptoms (what he called *Dauersymptome*), rather than re-enacting some whole traumatic episode or conjunction of episodes in a full-scale performance itself subject to further replay, as in the historic cases to be discussed below. By the early 1890s he already saw no difference among neuroses of whatever type (mainly hysterical or obsessional) with respect to such fundamentals as that, besides reconfiguring what he styled as traumatic material, they were always intermixed in some measure and were always, at bottom, sexual.[2] It was to these shared fundamentals that, in the late 1890s, he added an obligatory childhood original, and ultimately an infantile original, for every neurosis. I propose to show that he did so for reasons theoretical rather than empirical and that in so doing he cut himself off from all further insight into traumatic reliving, whether chronic or episodic, in the stricter and narrower sense of trauma, just when—paradoxically—he had opened the way to understanding it.

According to the traumatic theory of neurosis that was Freud's run-up to psychoanalysis, the traumatic material that neurotics were reliving was additive. Thus hysteria, as he put it in the context of his traumatic theory, "occurs only where [traumatic] events have piled up".[3] That is, some peculiarly painful or upsetting occurrence or circumstance, called a "precipitating event" or trigger trauma, would pull together lots of kindred, unassimilated traumatic material going back years or even decades in the depths of the sufferer's mind and would fashion it into composite, chronic symptoms. While in

[1]Freud (1940–1968): vol. XI, 284. Further: Binion (2003a): 238–39.
[2]Freud (1940–1968): vol. I, 258–59, 276. By "neurosis" here and elsewhere I mean, following Freud's usage, *psycho*neurosis as distinct from "*actual* neurosis", a chronic physical upset that Freud attributed to current sexual malfunction.
[3]Freud (1986): 284 (21 IX 1897).

his practice as he reported on it in letters to his close professional confidant of the time, Wilhelm Fliess, or in the volume of *Studies in Hysteria* that he co-authored with his senior neurological colleague Josef Breuer in 1895, one or another of those accumulated component traumas might well date from childhood or even infancy, this was a far cry from his later psychoanalytical theorem of a blueprint in infancy for every adult neurosis. His (originally Breuer's) so-called "cathartic" therapy of the time consisted in teasing the traumatic material behind the patient's symptoms out of oblivion or repression with the aid of hypnosis or, as a fall-back, suggestion, and then inviting the patient to recognize how he or, more usually, she was reliving that pathogenic material through those symptoms.[4] If the neurosis was curable, Freud held, such recognition would or should suffice to cure it.

A few examples from his own accounts of his practice will clarify the concepts and issues involved. The subject of his "first complete analysis of a hysteric",[5] an unwed youngest daughter caring with mounting discouragement for a depressive widowed mother, converted her sense of having come to a painful standstill in life into crippling leg pains. These drew primarily on earlier rheumatic pains, on the memory of having bandaged her late, stricken father's leg morning after morning while resting it on hers, and most recently on a tiring hike with a brother-in-law with whom she was secretly in love. It was after that hike that the dismal feeling of being stuck, of getting nowhere in life, came over her: hardly did she dismiss it from her mind as unworthy when it returned in body language. Concerning this last, quick conversion sequence, Freud remarked, stretching the key term beyond recognition: "Just such moments are the ones to be called 'traumatic'."[6] After a parting flare-up at Freud for having teased her secrets out of her, the patient wound up cured. In a comparable case of "traumatic summation",[7] a student singer choked off a whole middle pitch of her voice after having

[4]I write "inviting" rather than "getting" in view of Freud (1940–1968), vols. II–III, 113: "At that time [summer 1895] I considered ... that my task was accomplished when I had informed patients of the hidden meaning of their symptoms and that I was not responsible for whether or not they then accepted the solution."
[5]Freud (1940–1968): vol. I, 201.
[6]Freud (1940–1968): vol. I, 235.
[7]Freud (1940–1968): vol. I, 242.

all too long and too often swallowed her hate for an abusive father; some time later her fingertips started tingling when she angrily brushed away—as she graphically put it—the unbearable latest one of a lifelong series of unjust imputations against her by her elders.[8] In another young patient, a huge backlog of her father's sexual violence, real or imaginary, against her mother and herself crystallized into an obsessional neurosis after the gory climax of her seeing her mother bleed from the uterus.[9] Again, a young wife in treatment with him suffered from phobias that threw back to her elder sister's scary middle-of-the-night internment during their girlhood and, beyond that, to the guilty secret they shared of having once been sexually used together by their father.[10] Another patient got a head pain at age fifteen for fear of her grandmother's piercing gaze; the pain soon went into remission, only to recur as a fixed symptom before Freud's piercing gaze some thirty years later.[11] A spinster in his care suffered from fantasized taunts by neighbours about her having been jilted; the taunts reconfigured a repressed memory of a lodger's having suddenly thrust his penis into her hand without a follow-up.[12] And Freud traced yet another patient's melancholic sense of being worthless to her discovery at age fourteen that she had an imperforate hymen.[13]

In only the first of these sample cases, that of the crippling leg pains, did Freud claim a cure. He specified in *Studies in Hysteria* that by his cathartic method he could cure only acquired hysteria, hence by extension only acquired neuroses of whatever kind. In what he called his "model" case of acquired hysteria[14] the sufferer was a young Scottish governess in Austria whose widowed employer dashed her fond hopes of marrying him when he dumped on her in a rage for permitting a visitor to kiss his children in her care. Some months later he angrily forbade a cigar-smoking guest in turn to kiss them, whereupon the woman's sense of smell left her, replaced by an imaginary odour of cigar smoke. Her hysteria vanished when Freud brought home to her

---

[8] Freud (1940–1968): vol. I, 237–42.
[9] Freud (1986): vol. I, 312–15 (22 XII 1897).
[10] Freud (1940–1968): vol. I, 276–78 (literally, by "a certain masculine person").
[11] Freud (1940–1968): vol. I, 249.
[12] Freud (1986): vol. I, 107–09 (24 I 1895, Draft H).
[13] Freud (1986): vol. I, 373 (16 I 99).
[14] Freud (1940–1968): vol. I, 180.

how in her symptoms her employer's scolding of the cigar-smoker was fronting for his scolding of her, "the really operative trauma",[15] during which she had smelled precisely nothing for want of anything to smell. A comparable case, and presumable lightning cure, was that of an eighteen-year-old innkeeper's daughter he met while resting on a holiday hike. She suffered from gasping anxiety attacks through which, as he ascertained and explained, she was reliving two traumatic memories together: one of having fought her father off in bed at age fourteen without realizing at the time what he was up to, the other of having seen and heard him copulate with a cousin of hers a couple of years later.[16] By contrast, more dedicated hysterics might run him ragged when for every symptom he cured they would produce another,[17] on the order of the choked voice and tingling fingers of the aspirant singer. The first patient he treated by hypnosis would hystericize for any number of traumatic reasons simultaneously, generating stomach aches, leg stiffness, cramps, snorting, fear of strangers, animal phobias, and hallucinations galore along with a consuming hate for her newborn second daughter.[18] But what he called his "toughest and most instructive case of hysteria"[19] was that of the woman who developed a pain in the head from her grandmother's and later Freud's piercing gaze; she also got neck pains from swallowed insults, turned a rebuke that felt "like a slap in the face" into face pain, and massively literalized whatever pinched her heart or preyed on her mind; stretching it, she even managed to get her right hand to ache from worrying whether she could handle some new acquaintances right.[20] Inexhaustibly inventive, she took Freud through several hundred successive cycles of symptoms deciphered and dissolved one by one only to be replaced immediately afterwards.[21] Nor were hysterics unique in this; dyed-in-the-wool compulsives might likewise preserve their compulsiveness intact beneath any number of its malleable showings.

---

[15] Freud (1940–1968): vol. I, 179: "*das eigentlich wirksame Trauma*".

[16] Freud (1940–1968): vol. I, 184–95.

[17] Freud (1940–1968): vol. I, 259–64.

[18] Freud (1940–1968): vol. I, 99–162.

[19] Freud (1940–1968): vol. I, 245.

[20] Freud (1940–1968), vol. I, 244–51 (248: actually whether she would strike "*das rechte Auftreten*" with them).

[21] Freud (1940–1968), vol. I, 247 ("*mehrere Hunderte solcher Zyklen*"). Cf. Freud (1986): 326 (9 II 98): his hysteria cases were going "badly. I won't finish any of them this year either."

All through the 1890s Freud puzzled over whether a neurotic disposition might be innate or how one was otherwise acquired. On balance he tended to consider that even a one-shot neurosis, such as the Scottish governess's, presupposed a neurotic bent, and for that matter a specific neurotic bent, in her case hysterical.[22] Until late in the 1890s, he toyed with the idea that a neurotic potential was activated by sexual abstinence or aberration. By this latter he meant first and foremost masturbation current or even past (a puzzling insistent idea of his, for if all neurotics were masturbators, then masturbating did nothing to differentiate their symptoms), but also a use of condoms, withdrawal, and even coital excess.[23] In this vein he handily traced an old prude's fits of anxiety to hints at sex in her sheltered life[24] hard upon remarking that full cures were often possible when current sexual privation simply ceased.[25] But this line of actual sexual causality could not very well be stretched to cover much of his case load, scramble as he might to find sexual "noxae" in patients seemingly free of them.[26] Some of his sickest neurotics were happily married from way back, and to Breuer he peevishly conceded in 1896 that neurosis is possible "in persons who, to be sure, did not masturbate".[27] Besides, a sexual etiology of itself left the choice of neurotic type unexplained.

Meanwhile an alluring alternative to actual sexual frustration or aberration behind neurosis was suggested by indications of possible sexual abuse of Freud's neurotics in their earliest years with the traumatic impact on them delayed until after they reached sexual

---

[22]Freud (1940–1968): vol. I, 24–39 (1892–93 enclosures); 182–86 (1 III 96); etc.; Freud (1940–1968), I, 180, 231, 260–64, and so forth.

[23]Freud (1986): vol. I, 54 (27 XI 1893: coitus three times in a row) and *passim*; 71 (undated 1894 draft: "The neuroses: imbalances due to blocked discharge" and "Parallel of sexual and hunger neuroses"); 71–76 (undated 1894 draft: anxiety neurosis as due to current sexual tension or privation; ditto hysteria; melancholia too, though with love rather than sex missing and wanted); 86–87 (18 VIII 1894: still pushed current sexual abuse as the source of anxiety and other neurotic symptoms; also still stressed hereditary or constitutional predisposition, noting early masturbation and prior use of condoms); 90–91 (29 VIII 1894: more of the same); 96–102 (7 I 1895[?] draft on melancholia: ditto). Freud (1940–1968): I, 258: surmised sexual frustration behind all four cases he had just discussed in detail. Freud (1896): 312–13 (22 XII 1897: back to masturbation as the great source of hysteria and of all addiction).

[24]Freud (1940–1968): vol. I, 274–75.

[25]Freud (1940–1968): vol. I, 259–64.

[26]Freud (1986): vol. I, 68 (21 V 1894).

[27]Freud (1986): vol. I, 184 (1 III 96).

maturity. If only all neurosis originated in such passive victimization, in-born neurotic proclivities could be scrapped, and the issue of who acquired a neurotic disposition, indeed maybe even for which kind of neurosis, could be resolved. Freud speculated eagerly along these lines in the mid-1890s. "I sense the following strict precondition," he announced to Fliess in October 1895: "a primal (pre-pubertal) sexual experience with revulsion and fright for hysteria, with pleasure for obsessional neurosis".[28] He returned to the charge a week later, specifying that the pre-pubertal sexual traumas took pathogenic effect only after puberty and hence only "as memories".[29] The very next day he declared himself almost certain of his new schema, with neuroses and even neurotic dispositions both now curable on that basis.[30] He elaborated further on his felicitous construction after four more days,[31] and then reaffirmed its "basics" another eleven days later while also raising some doubt about "the pleasure-pain solution",[32] presumably because it reopened the old issue of proclivities in the new form of why such experiences gave pain to some children and pleasure to others. Quelling this unwelcome doubt, he ushered in the year 1896 with what, joshing himself, he called "A Christmas Tale": an extravagant comparison of hysteria, obsessional neurosis, and paranoia that led off from the need for a pre-pubertal sexual original of the precipitating cause in each case. A pre-pubertal trauma was harmful, he now specified, only as a memory reactivated by a similar experience at puberty and reinforced by an in-born disposition.[33] A few months later he even reworked this schema so that the ages for primal sexual traumas matched up with hysteria, obsessional neurosis, and paranoia respectively to make a tight deterministic bundle. "There is more speculation in it than usual," he conceded to Fliess.[34]

On this new theoretical high, Freud was claiming publicly by April 1896 that he had found pre-pubertal sexual abuse, typically at ages three or four, behind twelve female and six male neurotics all of whom he had cured accordingly "wherever circumstances

---

[28] Freud (1986): vol. I, 146 (8 X 95).
[29] Freud (1986): vol. I, 147 (15 X 1895).
[30] Freud (1986): vol. I, 148 (16 X 1895).
[31] Freud (1986): vol. I, 149–50 (20 X 1895).
[32] Freud (1940–1968): vol. I, 151–52 (31 X 1895).
[33] Freud (1986): vol. I, 169–78 (1 I 1896, enclosure).
[34] Freud (1986): vol. I, 201 (30 V 1896).

permitted".[35] He was to back off from this resounding claim in private some months later, considering above all that there was no telling reality from fantasy in the scenarios of early abuse that he had constructed out of his patients' fragmentary associations to their symptoms, but also that he had been unable to effect even a single "real" cure on that basis.[36] Not only did this last, private admission contradict his previous triumphant public claim; his previous triumphant public claim did not square with the public or private accounts he had given of his cases before 1896—any more for that matter than did his repeated affirmations in his later, psychoanalytical years that it was his patients who had kept steering him back to their early childhood. Of his four main and eight secondary cases, all female, discussed by him in sufficient detail in *Studies in Hysteria*, only two involved pubertal and two pre-pubertal material of whatever kind. And of those twelve plus eight other neuroses discussed adequately there and in subsequent letters to Fliess through 1899, only two drew on sexual experiences going back to puberty, another four to late childhood, and a single one to infancy. Still worse, this last one, which confirmed for Freud "the inherent authenticity of infantile traumas" even after his nominal about-face on that very issue, should sooner have strained his credulity even on his theoretical high, what with the patient claiming to remember that at six or seven months of age she had seen her mother nearly bleed to death from a sex wound inflicted by her father, that at two years of age she had been deflowered and infected with gonorrhea by the same penile offender, and that at age three she had witnessed a solo pantomime by her mother of fending off an anal-sexual assault in shrill protest.[37] With less blatant inconsequence he hailed one of the other cases of pre-pubertal abuse as "a new confirmation of the paternal etiology" (fathers being for him at that point the arch incestuous pedophiles) even though the old paternal abuse, far from

---

[35]Freud (1940–1968): vol. I, 414 (21 April 1896); cf. Freud., 364–65 and 398 (his totals varied, as did his gender and diagnostic breakdowns: see Esterson [1998]).

[36]Freud (1986): vol. I, 283–286 (21 IX 1897). He first recanted publicly in 1914, blaming patients' "reports" of early seduction instead of his own reconstructions: Freud (1940–1968): I (and, for bad measure, also blaming his "traumatic theory of hysteria", oddly ascribed to Charcot.)

[37]Freud (1986): vol. I, 314–15 (22 XII 1897).

festering under repression as required for traumatic effect, was fully conscious with the patient, affect inclusive, and on his own telling did not relate anyhow to her complaint of neurotic anxiety following from her brother's committal for insanity.[38] In one of his thirteen strictly post-pubertal cases of non-abuse, on the other hand, Freud regretted in so many words that "in all the patient's intimate disclosures to me the sexual element ... was completely lacking".[39] The indications are that the radical turn in his thinking of the late 1890s to childhood sexual trauma as the source of neurosis was not fact- but theory-driven, the facts themselves being reshaped by theory even as the theorist slept through many a consultation.[40] To round out the record, the three psychoanalytical case histories that he was to publish in later years (Dora, the Rat Man, and the Wolf Man) famously showed him steering the patients' thoughts back to sex in childhood whenever they went their own way instead.[41]

Before he began speculating about early sexual abuse behind neurosis, Freud had seen childhood traumas as mere items in an associative series with no causal value even collectively unless and until they were catalyzed by a "precipitating event" later in life and thereby enlisted into symptomatic service, like those cumulative hates that his aspirant singer hurt her voice swallowing. With his child abuse schema, on the contrary, the causal onus shifted to early sexual traumas presaging future neuroses that would, though, remain in abeyance until some critical moment after puberty even while gathering lesser traumatic material into their orbit in the interim. This childhood impetus to a neurosis, albeit an impetus hanging fire, made the remote personal past actual. Previously Freud had considered that unconscious material could sustain a neurosis only if, however old, it had continuing existential

---

[38] Freud (1986): vol. I, 251–52 (28 IV 1897). In later years he was to suppose that consciously remembered abuse fronted for previous unremembered abuse real or imaginary.

[39] Freud (1940–1968): vol. I, 160.

[40] Freud (1986): vol. I, 331 (15 III 1898): "I sleep during my afternoon analyses."

[41] Szecsödy (1998): vol. I, 74 ("he constantly pressed Dora to confirm his impressions and interpretations"); Künstlicher (1998): 154 ("he was guided more by his wish to confirm his theory than by the Rat Man's analytical material"); Fish (1989): 543 (he practiced "persuasion ... on a massive scale" with the Wolf Man). On his "highly coercive and directive technique" as applied in the 1890s: Esterson (1998): 5–7.

relevance. Thus the innkeeper's daughter was anxiously gasping in current fear of her father for having tattled on him to her mother, while conversely a massage and light hypnosis sufficed to cure a former singer whose jaws had been locked nearly shut for years from causes that were by then "evidently long since done and over with".[42] On the child abuse construction, by contrast, traumatic material no longer obsolesced. At the same time, on that construction as before, a childhood sex trauma could take neurotic effect in later life only as an unconscious memory: no change here. This no-change enabled Freud to put the child abuse construction to rest all the more easily, memory alone being operant whether true or false—child abuse or no. By the same token, however, he implicitly and implausibly equated early scary sex phantasms with actual early sex traumas. He did so as well on the connected ground that imaginary child abuse could not be told apart from real child abuse as reconstructed by him (precious few sex traumas or phantasms from later childhood, let alone infancy, were recollected by his patients themselves). The upshot was that to his mind a false memory might pack as much wallop as a true memory, however long it had bided its traumatic time in abeyance. On this reckoning a girl would be equally prone to develop a guilt neurosis in later life if she had enjoyed being used by her father sexually or if she had only enjoyed imagining it. At the same time, in imputing to the fantasizing child an active role in acquiring a neurosis, Freud reopened the whole question of neurotic disposition, now recast as the question of which children tended to fantasize to future neurotic effect, and then to neurotic effect of which kind.

If Freud's about-face on sex abuse in childhood as the stock source of neurosis was not as pinpointed in time as is commonly held, neither was it as pivotal in theory. He might still invoke his failed rule of child sex abuse behind every trauma some months after he had professedly scrapped it.[43] Much more importantly, even after he did finally scrap it he still stuck to the childhood source of every neurosis, sex abuse or no. It is this sticking point that was fundamental for

---

[42] Freud (1940–1968): vol. I, 237n: "*offenbar längst abgetan*".

[43] Freud (1986): vol. I, 312 (12 XII 1897: "my confidence in the paternal etiology has gone way up"), 314 (22 XII 1897: "the inherent authenticity of infantile traumas").

his transition to psychoanalysis proper: the childhood origin, next the childhood original, and soon afterwards the infantile original, of all neurosis. At first, in his letter to Fliess nominally writing off sex abuse in childhood as the single source of neurosis, he had reported himself ready to give up on two things along with it: on "the complete cure of a neurosis and the certain knowledge of its etiology in childhood".[44] In the event he did not give up on either. His about-face should logically have put him back where he had been before: with some tenacious neuroses deriving from childhood, even from sex abuse in childhood, but also some neuroses being first acquired in adulthood, these being the most amenable to cure, and some being due to inveterate, in-born neurotic dispositions incurable by his methods.

However, rather than back off from the childhood source of neurosis with its irresistible built-in suggestion of deepest roots, he took a gigantic new step forward in that same direction over the following months and years. He part-discerned and part-contrived a normative schema of child development by psychosexual stages, with an inherent risk of a potentially pathogenic emotional fixation at one or another stage in case too little or too much gratification were forthcoming there. In the final reckoning, his infantile stages were to be narcissistic first and then predominantly oral, anal, and phallic by turns, with sex play and sex fantasies at every stage, and with a potential for psychosis, hysteria, and obsession respectively in the event of a hang-up at one of the first three stages.[45] Traumatic experiences at any point might also carry their own neurotic potential, particularly at the phallic stage, culminating in the emotionally charged "Oedipus complex" with its built-in castration fear and its visions of parental intercourse soon mythified as the "primal scene". (The "Oedipus complex" evidently popped up in Freud's practice of the time, but the clincher for him was its [guest?] appearance in his self-analysis of the late 1890s: to Fliess he reported that he had found it "in myself too", adding immodestly: "and now take

---

[44]Freud (1986): vol. I, 284 (21 IX 1897).

[45]For a hysteric's oral fixation as it first came into his practice explicitly, see Freud (1986): vol. I, 232–33 (3 I 1897), and likewise for a compulsive's anal fixation, see Freud (1986): 313–14 (22 XII 1897). But not until about 1900 was his new schema roughly complete.

it to be a universal event of early childhood".)[46] This new schema eliminated the need for an in-born neurotic predisposition in case there was no such thing: developmental disturbances could be held accountable for all manner of neurotic affliction. It also systematized the distinction between an acquired neurotic disposition and an acquired neurosis: the stronger a fixation on an infantile sexual aim, the less of a later reverse or frustration was needed for a neurosis to result. Finally—and this is the crucial point—on these new schematic terms no neurotic potential could be acquired in infancy, whether by trauma or by fixation, without a premonitory neurosis already ensuing in infancy, for any infantile trauma or fixation strong enough to generate an adult neurosis by delayed action was perforce symptomatic from the start. In Freud's own formulation: "When a neurosis breaks out in later life, analysis invariably shows it to be a direct continuation of that infantile neurosis."[47] He saw to it that this was so in the analyses that he himself performed from there on out.

No adult neurosis without its infantile original: this new rule of Freud's had its supportive counterpart in the prodigious theory of dreams that he developed along with his psychoanalytical theory of neurosis. The dream "contains *in nuce* the whole psychology of the neuroses," he told Fliess along the way.[48] Just as on his psychoanalytical terms an adult neurosis conjoined an infantile original with a recent "precipitating event", so too in his dream theory did a dream encode both together a disturbing thought pushed out of mind the day before and an infantile wish that the dream depicted as fulfilled. Despite this two-tier dynamic that he postulated in dreams and in neuroses alike, Freud accentuated the infantile in both cases. As he told Fliess in 1898, "Dream life seems to me to derive entirely from the residues of the prehistoric period of life (ages 1–3)—the same period which ... alone contains the etiology of all the psychoneuroses. ... A recent wish leads to a dream only if it can link up with material from this prehistoric period ... if [it] is an offspring of a prehistoric wish or can get itself adopted by one."[49] Likely his rule

[46] Freud (1986): 293 (15 X 1897).
[47] Freud (1940–1968): vol. XI, 378.
[48] Freud (1986): 273 (7 VII 1897).

of infantile origination went from neuroses to dreams even if it is unclear which of the two emergent, mutually reinforcing theories influenced the other more. Whereas his child abuse theorem dates from the spring of 1896, he did not relegate the wish function of dreams to their infantile component until 1898, when he did so by express analogy with the neuroses.[50] He did so hesitantly in the first instance, moreover, and for many years in the abstract only. "The wish represented in a dream must be an infantile one," he asserted flatly just once in *The Interpretation of Dreams*, completed in 1899, only to add some pages later that, whereas repressed sexual wishes from infancy "furnish the motive force for the formation of all psychoneurotic symptoms", he would "leave it open whether sexual and infantile factors are required by the theory of dreams as well".[51] Theory notwithstanding, the dreams that Freud recounted from first to last appear to have originated in every case not in the infantile unconscious, but in the previous day's preoccupations (except the typical dreams, these being children's dreams that recur in adulthood), besides often dragging in associated material from other ages since infancy; or perhaps more properly put, such earlier post-infantile material often linked up with the main dream thought, whether to help disguise it or just to get in on the act. This awkward disconnect between theory and reality may be why he mostly confined his specimen dream analyses in *The Interpretation of Dreams* to their latent contents drawn from the dreamer's previous day's experience. He nonetheless insisted dogmatically until near the end of his days on the infantile source of all dreams, and even in rescinding that infantile edge *in extremis* in his unfinished *Outline of Psychoanalysis* through the even-handed formulation: "dreams from the ego or from the id",[52] he retained the formula that dreams are wish fulfilments, which of itself lent the infantile component a manner of overweight as the source of those wishes that the dream represented

[49] Freud (1986): 329–30 (10 III 1898, stress added).
[50] Freud (1986): 329–30 (10 III 1898).
[51] Freud (1940–1968): vols II–III, 559, 611. Further, 611: "I have already taken a step well beyond what can be proven in assuming that the dream-wish invariably derives from the unconscious." Cf. Freud (1986): 330 (10 III 1898): "how far I shall be able to adhere to this all-out theory ... is still uncertain", and Freud (1940–1968): II–III, 194–224, especially 223–24.
[52] Freud (1940–1968): vol. XVII, 88 ("*Träume vom Ich her oder vom Es her*").

as fulfilled. So comparably as of the late 1890s did he see the infantile source of neuroses as determinative and the "precipitating event" as merely accessory (despite some telltale concessions in particular cases). Aligning neuroses with dreams for a change, he declared hysterical, and probably all neurotic, symptoms to be wish fulfilments,[53] which was easier to see for an innkeeper's daughter gasping over forbidden sex than for an aspirant singer choking on old hates. And in practice he himself mostly supplied the infantile component of dreams as of neuroses with or without the dreamer's or patient's acquiescence. An egregious instance of such imposed interpreting is the prime object lesson on how dreams work that he gave in his closing course of university lectures of 1915–1917.[54] There the dreamer saw herself with her husband in a half-empty theatre after having rushed to buy tickets at what proved to be too high a price. The latent dream thought from the day before, which the dreamer readily conceded, was that she had made a bad bargain by rushing into marriage, symbolized by being in the theatre. Years later Freud supplied the infantile wish shown in the dream as gratified: to see what goes on in marriage. But as Stephen Kern put it: "Infants do not wish to see what goes on in marriage. Perhaps children do."[55] In any case, it was no insistence by dreamers but rather the architectonics of Freud's dream theory in sync with his theory of neurosis that mandated an infantile wish fulfilled by every dream.

With his requirement of an infantile original for every neurosis, the theorist Freud painted the therapist into a corner. The hunt for infantile underpinnings of neuroses was perforce futile where the symptoms were fluid, as with his patient who kept literalizing the likes of a piercing gaze, or again with committed neurotics like the Wolf Man, half-persuaded by Freud after over four years of analysis that his neurotic trouble came at age one-and-a-half from a traumatic peep at parental intercourse performed *a tergo* three times running: pronounced cured by Freud in 1914, he spent his remaining sixty-five years generating ever-new symptoms, only to

---

[53] Freud (1986): 377–78 (19 II 1899).

[54] Freud (1940–1968): vol. XI, 120–23, 225–26, 230–32.

[55] Stephen Kern, private communication. In *The Interpretation of Dreams* Freud had analysed this dream for its preconscious contents only: Freud (1940–1968): vols. II–III, 418–20.

wind up calling psychoanalysis the bunk. And with self-made as against born neurotics, what need was there for an Ur-neurosis to explain the depressive fit of a fourteen-year-old on learning that she had an imperforate hymen? The hunt for such an infantile original would only have provided a therapeutic distraction in Freud's practice of the 1890s. As late as his last university lectures he conceded the point implicitly, by a sort of Freudian slip, in regard to a wife's compulsive ritual of summoning her maid on one pretext or another while standing beside a soiled tablecloth: there was no need to recur to childhood in this case, he told his students, since the symptom threw back no farther than to her wedding night, when her husband had stained their bed sheets with red ink lest the maid notice that he had proved impotent.[56] Besides, in none of the cases he reported in the 1890s did the post-infantile traumas he then identified as "operative" fail to explain the symptoms: all were neat fits. And were the cures he then claimed unreal? Of his twelve sufficient case reports in *Studies in Hysteria*, two were stated cures, another four presumable cures, and a further two possible cures.[57] As late as January 1899 he claimed to Fliess to have cured a hysterical melancholia acquired from a trauma at age fourteen, and this with no mention of recourse to earlier childhood.[58] True, in 1914 he pronounced his perennial patient the Wolf Man cured who in fact had a veritable lifetime of neurotic relapse ahead of him. But that false cure, which turned on a suppositional "primal scene", only highlights by contrast his conclusion to his case history of the patient who had come to him in 1893 with crippling leg pains brought on by her disavowed feeling of being trapped in life: within months he rejoiced to see her dancing away at a house party, then to learn of her love-marriage shortly afterwards.[59] Conversely, his 1890s concept of summation, whereby it took a "precipitating event" at the end of the line to catalyze a whole run of traumatic precedents and distil symptoms out of them, made no provision for an "operative" infantile trauma even where exceptionally there was one. He might, however, ignore

[56] Freud (1940–1968): vol. XI, 271.

[57] He also called a sketchily reported thirteenth case a cure: Freud (1940–1968): vol. I, 138n.

[58] Freud (1986): 373 (16 I 1899).

[59] Freud (1940–1968): vol. I, 226.

this last-straw concept in practice at the time, as when he nicely derived a woman's compulsive idea that her sewing class mustn't end yet, that she wasn't done yet, from her grandmother's harsh strictures against her leaving the potty before her business there was finished.[60] On Freud's couch in the 1890s, infantile originals were rightly reserved for symptoms acquired in infancy.

In sum, Freud's psychoanalytical rule of a childhood original for every adult symptom or neurosis brought him only mixed theoretical and therapeutic gain. On the down side in particular—and this is the central point at issue here—it ruled out traumatic reliving, in which an unprecedented, shattering experience is re-experienced close to the bone in all its haunting specificity. That re-experience might be chronic, as with nagging memories or transparent nightmares constituting a so-called traumatic neurosis, nicknamed shell shock in World War I and its aftermath. In his late, unfinished *Outline of Psychoanalysis* Freud reiterated his standing ground rule of neurotic origination—"in every case the later neurotic illness links up with the prelude in childhood"—only to add this time: "The so-called traumatic neuroses (due to excessive fright or severe somatic shocks ...) may be an exception; their connection to determinants in childhood has so far eluded detection."[61] True, he cancelled this nominal concession by tacking on the implication that those childhood determinants were no less real for being elusive,[62] but no matter: he was not hot on their trail. A still bigger casualty of his theorem of the infantile neurotic precedent than the traumatic neurosis was episodic traumatic reliving such as makes history. For the trauma that gets relived episodically, as a full-length event, is a trauma properly so-called that in almost every case strikes out of the blue like a sudden blow on the head (as it does literally in Pirandello's paradigmatic *Henry IV*).[63] When it strikes that way, it strikes with no lead time for anxiety, as Freud later stressed,[64] but above all with no precedents to help its victim cope. To be sure, it may

---

[60] Freud (1986): 313 (22 XII 1897).

[61] Freud (1940–1968): vol. XVII, 111.

[62] This last was his stock point: Freud (1940–1968): vol. XI, 283–84.

[63] A signal exception was Pierre Janet's patient Irène: traumatized by her mother's slow death in her care, she would re-enact it in a trance-like state with a phantom mother whenever she saw an empty bed. See Janet (1911): 507–44; Janet (1919): 268–75; Janet (1920): 39–40; Janet (1928): 205–15.

[64] Freud (1940–1968): vol. XIII, 31–32.

link up with earlier upsets as it strains for precedents in the course of the reliving, but that is something else.

In 1914 Freud coined the term "repetition compulsion" (*Wiederholungszwang*) to cover patients in analysis acting out feelings or attitudes from their infancy that were never clearly conscious: such, he astutely observed, was their way of remembering.[65] The term "repetition compulsion" carries a deceptive ring of affinity with episodic traumatic reliving, from which, however, such acting out differs radically in at least three ways: it is elicited by the analysis rather than contrived spontaneously; it reproduces a diffuse cluster of inchoate relations to the surrounding world rather than a single, structured traumatic event; and above all, in episodic reliving as a rule not the trauma itself, but only its reliving, is unconscious. In 1920 Freud relaunched the "repetition compulsion" in the new guise of an instinctive losing effort by the human organism to inure itself to excessive stimuli.[66] He observed this tendency at work first in his baby grandson repeatedly tossing away and pulling back a toy held by a string, then in the recurrent stark memories that characterize a traumatic neurosis, only to wind up inferring from it a death drive inherent in all life[67]—none of which even began to approach episodic traumatic reliving. By contrast, what more than approached episodic traumatic reliving was when his first hypnotic patient repeated his treatment of her serially with other doctors, symptoms inclusive, beginning a few years after she left his care—or so he learned in 1924, noting: "It was the true 'repetition compulsion'"[68], which to my mischievous mind suggests that he saw the "true

---

[65]Freud (1940–1968): vol. X, 129–30.

[66]Freud (1940–1968): vol. XIII, 17–22.

[67]For Freud's death drive historicized, see Binion (1994a): 17–23; Binion (1995); and Binion (1994b): 117–24. In this usage Freud meant by "repetition compulsion" an aim inherent in instincts to restore a former state of things: Freud (1940–1968): XII, 251. In Freud (1920): XIV, 150, he invoked cryptically the frequent aim of a neurosis to undo a traumatic experience: "What did not turn out in the desired way is undone in another way through repetition" ("*Was nicht in solcher Weise geschehen ist, wie es dem Wunsch gemäß hätte geschehen sollen, wird durch die Wiederholung in anderer Weise ungeschehen gemacht*"). His dark logic here appears to have been that, as instincts are all repetitious with the ultimate aim of undoing the traumatic intrusion of life on the peace of death, the aim of any and all traumatic repetition must be to undo the trauma behind it.

[68]Freud (1940–1968): vol. I, 162n ("*Es war der richtige 'Wiederholungszwang'*").

'repetition compulsion'" in episodic rather than chronic reliving (besides allowing that his failed cure was traumatic) even while now distancing himself from the dubious concept by the use of quotation marks.

Why should the victim of a painful trauma keep remembering it? Freud's best answer was: in order to be thrown by it less. A trauma hits too fast to arouse anxiety, he argued; anxiety tags after a trauma when the trauma hits but then precedes the trauma when it is remembered; thanks to this latter "signal anxiety", its victim braces for it in remembrance and thereby dulls its impact.[69] On this construction, all hurtful traumas would arouse anxiety. In fact, however, some elicit only other affects—shame, disgust, compassion, disaffection, disenchantment, whatever. More to the point, Freud's tacit premise was that traumas hurt even when they are off the mind, or else why remember them in order to dull their impact? Not that they hurt unconsciously—there is no unconscious hurting; what hurts, not the hurting itself, is off the mind. But Freud stressed the conscious over the unconscious in traumatic shock: the ego, caught off guard by a trauma, seeks to gain control over it. His tacit premise alone holds: traumas do go on hurting even when they are off the mind. For the rest, if a trauma has aroused anxiety, anxiety will precede it in memory only insofar as the memory is expected to be traumatic, in which case it is the remembered trauma that brings on the anxiety after all. Or more simply put, anxiety doesn't signal a trauma if remembering the trauma is what arouses the anxiety. As for such niceties as whether the pain of remembering a trauma is the old pain resurfacing or a new one, he never addressed them. His best explanation for repeating a trauma, transposed from remembering a trauma, would logically have been likewise: to gain control over it. But a trauma is not itself controlled in being replayed; what is controlled is only the form of the replay. Traumatic reliving was just not Freud's forte after 1900.

By way of explaining the castration complex, which he saw as endemic to infantile psychosexuality, Freud postulated an archaic inborn memory trace of a castrating tribal father of yore traumatically gang-murdered by a band of his sons who then relived their grave deed ritually in a totemic ceremony prefiguring all future

[69]Freud (1940–1968): vol. XIII, 31–32; vol. XIV, 199–200; vol. XV, 100–01; vol. XVII, 130.

religious observance.[70] This conception of a collective analogue to an individual obsessional neurosis fed into the historical fantasy of Freud's last years whereby the Jews of the Exodus murdered Moses in re-enactment of the age-old murder of the fabled tribal father, whereupon a couple of millennia later the Jews of Judea in turn had Jesus crucified in re-enactment of the murder of Moses.[71] With this grandiose conception of a collective re-enactment of two world-historical mass traumas by turns at countless generations' remove in each case, Freud made ample figurative (not to say fanciful) amends for his exclusion of episodic traumatic reliving from his psychoanalytical framework and, correspondingly, from a theoretical passage on traumatic reliving in that selfsame work on Moses.[72]

Now to sum up. In Freud's traumatic theory of the 1890s, neurosis was a chronic reliving of traumas loosely defined. In his later, stricter usage, the chronic reliving of a trauma proper, or lasting massive upset, was a special kind of neurosis: the traumatic neurosis. He pointed the way to understanding episodic as well as chronic reliving when he showed in the 1890s that all neurotic symptoms were relivings. But then he blocked the traumatic neurosis, or chronic reliving of a trauma proper, out of his psychoanalytical system when he adopted the rule of an infantile original behind every neurosis, for the distinctive feature of true-blue traumas is that they have no originals. Episodic reliving for its part had no access to his system by the same token and, further, in that it was not neurotic. Not being neurotic, it never entered his consulting room, so that he never dealt with it clinically. Yet his decipherment of symptomatic behaviour as remembrance in action was precisely suited to make sense of episodic traumatic reliving. As a phrase, the "repetition compulsion" that he postulated in 1914 and redefined in 1920 might have seemed to denote, or at least to cover, episodic traumatic reliving, but as a mechanism it was unrelated and even incompatible. Late in his life, in spite of his psychoanalytic schema inhospitable to episodic traumatic reliving, Freud fantasized a massive case of it

---

[70] Freud (1940–1968): vol. IX, 26–121. In 1930 Freud (1940–1968), vol. XIV, 422–23, qualified this last generalization in consideration of an "oceanic feeling" of universal oneness underlying religiosity outside of father-religions.

[71] Freud (1940–1968): vol. XVI, 101–246.

[72] Freud (1940–1968): vol. XVI, 180–81.

extending from the hypothesized murder of a primeval tribal father (itself relived symptomatically meanwhile as totemic ritual) through the supposed murder of Moses to the real crucifixion of Christ. The psychohistorian's task is to replace such pseudohistory by history with the same Freudian aim of uncovering its inner workings. To that task I turn next.

CHAPTER THREE

Reliving in history

Traumas that are relived are not themselves relivings. On the contrary, they normally strike out of the blue[1] with no precedents that leap to mind to help their victims cope. Or so I asserted a few pages ago in my rundown of Freud's trouble conceptualizing trauma and especially schematizing its aftermath. That aftermath may include episodic reliving of the trauma, but this is not the clinician's business, for it is not seen or felt as a sickness by those who unwittingly engage in it; indeed, it is not seen or felt by them at all. How traumas get relived episodically—or for short, how they get relived[2]—is best known from history. Such historical knowledge is the subject of this chapter. I propose to approach that subject through some historic cases of traumatic reliving that I have studied in depth over the past decades, and first off through the case best suited to turn the page on Freud in that the traumatic experience involved ought by all Freudian rights to have thrown back

[1]But see ch. 2, n. 63, on Janet's Irène.

[2]That is, the term "reliving" alone will henceforth denote outright re-staging or re-enactment as against other ways of reliving trauma such as haunting recall or phobic defence.

to Freud's own preferred infantile hang-up but didn't. In this very case, which he himself explored from close up, Freud took the infantile original of the experience for granted only to miss the traumatic impact of that experience altogether.

Imagine a little girl who courts her father unsuccessfully. As Freud came to see it when he laid the foundations of psychoanalysis, such failed courtship is the rule for normal little girls and proper fathers. Imagine further that this particular little girl grows up to meet a learned, seer-like older man with a magical power of words who takes her on as a disciple and shows a human, all too human, attraction to her besides. She leads him on while boasting right and left that he is after her. Her juvenile chatter reaches his sensitive ears. Overreacting, he tells her off in a vicious rage. She pretends to herself that she doesn't much care—that the fine airs he had put on with her only covered his dirty designs on her. Yet his harsh break with her and crude put-down of her haunt her innermost thoughts. She becomes a writer whose fiction turns around and around that rattling episode in various thick or thin disguises without her ever quite realizing it. After a time she also re-enacts the episode unwittingly again and again in real life, herself playing the sage mentor with younger lovers slated for dumping, hence with the original roles and terms of erotic engagement in simple reverse.

When she recounts or replays the episode in disguise, she does so in exact conformity with it alone and not with any infantile original behind it. Hence to all appearances her insatiable need to relive, first in fantasy and then also in actuality, her misadventure with her towering, touchy master derived entirely from that misadventure itself. To understand her need to relive, does it matter, then, whether in that misadventure her fancied suitor was a father figure? It should matter the less since, in the Freudian perspective, any older man whom a woman leads on is by that very token a father figure, whereas not every put-down by a father figure gets relived—far from it. Besides, this woman's father had been both aloof and gentle with her in her childhood, whereas her mentor first got under her skin and then gave her a brutal brush-off. Indeed, his intimation of intimacy so rudely rescinded was the trauma that she afterwards relived; otherwise there was none. The childhood precedent may help to explain why she led her older man on and then claimed that he was after her; it gives no hint of why she later incessantly relived the fiasco that ensued.

I have said that our little girl's failed courtship of her father in childhood was a Freudian golden rule. But is that Freudian gold solid? I took for granted that it was even when, in my *Frau Lou*, I nonetheless played down the paternal precedent after reconstructing Lou Salomé's brush with Friedrich Nietzsche as just recounted.[3] Since then, older and bolder, I have come to question that precedent itself, the frustrated father romance, as every little girl's fated lot. As far as Freud's records disclose, none of his female neurotics remembered it themselves in treatment; he supplied the missing memory for them all. And once he established his so-called Oedipus Complex both male and female as a touchstone of psychoanalysis,[4] it could no longer be disconfirmed within psychoanalysis, whereas it is inaccessible through any other medium. Even granting its universality, however, wasn't it by that very token extraneous to the specific trauma that Frau Lou relived?

Lou initially pushed the limits of denial of her trauma when she omitted Nietzsche from her diary retrospect on the year of their encounter and break-up: 1882. Two years later she fashioned a girlish novel around their three get-togethers[5]: three self-identified characters agonize, and two of them perish, in deathly gloom over their three failed romances with the single Nietzsche persona. Her defining trauma showed less nakedly, if no less starkly, through her later fiction. One striking specimen, her short story "Geschwister" ("Siblings") of 1919, even made excuses for her traumatizer.[6] In it, a little darling sneak-visits a shady guru a couple of times with a wicked thrill, only to be pushed downstairs by him on arriving for a third visit. In the thick of her fit of frightful shock and panic that ensues she learns that he was out of control in thus brutalizing her because he was about to be *seized*, or taken into custody. Far from sympathizing, she exults, for he had not *repelled her* after all. After Nietzsche was doubly seized in 1889—that is, taken into custody in a fit of madness—she posed in print as his enduring philosophic and personal confidante. When her bluff was called (first off by his sister),

[3] Binion (1968): 35–111 and passim.
[4] He did so at the Munich psychoanalytical congress of 1913. I write "his" and "so-called" advisedly: see further Binion (1968): 7–20 ("The Trouble with Oedipus").
[5] Andreas-Salomé, (1885).
[6] Andreas-Salomé (1921); further, Binion (1968): 416–38 and passim.

she declined to respond in public, alleging discretion about her private traffic with him—including, she whispered, a hapless bid by him for her hand. It was about when she confected this courtship by Nietzsche that she began her real-life reliving. She relived at as lively a pace off paper as on, as if galvanized by that very purpose, alternating her matronly love life on the loose with bouts of writing at home in a white marriage to a philologist of Nietzsche's stamp and vintage. In her best-documented off-paper reliving, the established, mature author Lou Andreas-Salomé latched onto a lyrically effusive youngster, firmed up his thinking and writing in three intimate encounters geared to her Nietzsche chronology, even changed his name from René to Rainer Maria Rilke, then cast him off in due course as a "neurotic homunculus"[7]: his remote dependence on her ever after fed the glory of German letters. Her traumatic mechanics with their alternation of writing and doing were by no means unexampled. Thus the Italian playwright Luigi Pirandello drew one stage play after another out of his real-life drama of having had his wife committed when she once traumatically found him all too close to their daughter, and he relived that family drama offstage in reverse through an open but chaste affair with an actress he called his "elective daughter" upon disinheriting her fleshly predecessor in her favour.[8]

Was Lou's reliving typical? For a first shot at a normal course of reliving if there is one, I propose to jump the gun and schematize Lou's case as normative, then right the resultant wrongs afterwards in the light of other historic cases. The most salient aspect of Lou's reliving was, in its active phase, how very successfully she plied the world around her to her unsuspected traumatic purpose. The human accessories to her reliving, the junior partners on whom she set her sights, were all wholly compliant. And she used them as if she were herself yielding to fate—as if the choice were no more hers than theirs. She recorded no scruples over (in her euphemism) restoring them "to the all" when, by her traumatic calendar, their

[7]Binion (1968): 300.

[8]I reconstruct Pirandello's personal drama in Binion (1981b): 127–53. "Drama" is the recurrent word for it in *Six Characters in Search of an Author*. To be exact, under Italian law he could disinherit his legal daughter for his "elective daughter" (Marta Abba) only halfway.

time was up. She did, though, preserve some epistolary tokens of their heartbreak that followed—so many flip-side counterparts to her fake shrug at Nietzsche's rejection of her. Although her trauma itself had been as much of her own making as were its later re-runs, she betrayed precious little guilt over it either when she incurred it or later when she relived it whether in fact or fancy. Nor did her episodic relivings involve any escalation of the original outcome[9] or any effort to forestall that fated finale. She frequently ransacked her childhood and youth for precedents to her trauma as if to tell herself by implication that it was nothing much new—that *it* was the rehash. In several reminiscences in her journal in particular she fashioned a pulpit philosopher who had prepared her for confirmation into a forerunner of Nietzsche, failed marriage proposal and all. Then in her late-life discipleship to Freud she harked back to her father as her aboriginal god-man. Even so, she had toed the straight traumatic line in all of her tireless reliving and reloving. Or had she?

For starters, not all relivings are so direct a transposition of their traumatic originals. Hers, fictional and factual alike, were all aligned faithfully point for point with the trauma behind them except for the single, real-life switch from chaste tutee to unchaste tutor. At the opposite extreme, Otto von Bismarck's reliving in power politics of a seminal trauma out of his youth was as crooked as they come. To highlight its deviousness, I propose to reproduce and then emend a brief account of it that I once published in a psychohistorical journal. This account told the inside story of the so-called "Bismarck system" in diplomacy accurately enough, yet for all its accuracy it pointed to the wrong conclusion, as readers' feedback brought home to me. Here it is.[10]

Otto von Bismarck was for his own times, and has remained, the personification of *Realpolitik*—of naked, calculating power politics. His proudest claim to fame as *Realpolitiker* was to have united the German states outside of Austria in 1870–1871. He did so through a victorious war that, as Prussian chancellor, he manipulated the French into provoking over a German candidate to succeed a deposed queen of Spain, Isabella II. After this crowning stunt, he dominated European diplomacy for the next two decades as the

[9]Her *fictional* relivings did, however, involve some (as did Pirandello's).
[10]Almost verbatim from Binion (2005a): 25–26.

newly proclaimed German Emperor's so-called Iron Chancellor, contriving and maintaining an intricate network of alliances binding all the other European powers except France directly or indirectly to Germany. Indeed, the rationale of his complex diplomatic design was to keep France from finding support for a possible war to recover Alsace–Lorraine, annexed by Germany as war booty in 1871. After this annexation he realized only too well that the new German Empire, for all its military might, was permanently at risk in that any European power could threaten it confident of French support. At statesmanly nerves' edge in consequence, he sought to tranquilize the rest of Europe. Thus he restrained as best he could the German proponents of state backing for commercial or colonial expansion. Thus too in 1878, a dangerous crisis having arisen in the Balkans, he defused it through an international conference that he convened and ran as "honest broker". But above all he conducted a personal, and in crucial respects secretive, diplomacy of often contradictory foreign alliances for mutual assistance or desistance in case of war—the first such standing peacetime alliances in history. Of this diplomatic juggling Emperor William I is often said to have remarked that only Bismarck could balance four or five balls at once in mid-air while riding horseback. Bismarck himself was the source of the familiar diagnosis of him as suffering from (in its usual French formulation) a "*cauchemar des alliances*"—an alliance nightmare.

Clearly a twenty-year running nightmare smacks of pathology. That in private the Iron Chancellor was an insomniac, a hypochondriac, a glutton, a morphine addict, and lots else in this vein is no news. But was his *Realpolitik* itself fed from subrational depths, as his calling it a nightmare suggests? And if so, what was the latent stuff of that running nightmare?

To begin with, Bismarck's *cauchemar des alliances* bespoke a morbid defensiveness against a real danger. To his credit as statesman, he saw that real danger and defended against it effectively, albeit compulsively. To his discredit as statesman, however, he had failed to foresee it, or at all odds to forestall it, although it was clear to him right after his new Empire conjured it up: as early as August 1871 he was calling the annexation of Lorraine in particular a mistake. This is no doubt why he took the danger so personally. His nightmare amounted, then, to a guilty anxiety lest a self-identified Imperial Germany risk disaster in the European power play.

That Bismarck was complicit in putting Germany at risk and then took that risk tormentedly to heart suggests that there was a biographic referent for his defensive *cauchemar des alliances* such as underlies all good nightmares—a personal disaster that he was frenetically guarding against after the fact. To repeat, his system of alliances, continually reaffirmed, renewed, and reinforced, was designed to debar any and every party to it from a rapprochement with revanchist France. Once "alliance" is understood in its original, dynastic sense of marriage, then Bismarck's personal precedent for his nightmarish fear of a hostile alliance and of his country's ruination, the traumatic origin of his *cauchemar des alliances*, is evident.

In 1837, twenty-two-year-old Bismarck, then a Prussian civil servant stationed in Aachen, was madly smitten with an English beauty of seventeen touring abroad with her parents: Isabella Loraine.[11] Hitherto dutiful and frugal, he deserted his post for months on end to tag after the girl in France, gambled himself deep into debt in hopes of matching her family's affluence, and even gave out a date for their prospective marriage in England, only to wind up jilted for a rival. This courtship-and-casino fiasco left him with a broken heart and, it seemed, a broken career, plus debts that cost him years of labour thereafter on his run-down family estate in Pomerania to repay.[12] In letters he recounted the devastating double disaster with bitter humour to one friend just afterwards and to another in 1845, and he reminisced about it moodily to his wife in 1851. Nor did he put it behind him even then; instead, true to post-traumatic form, it returned to haunt him long years afterwards. Its return was surely facilitated, if not actually elicited, by the coincidence that the Spanish crisis was touched off by a second Isabella, and again that the French name for the most problematic, un-Germanic chunk of German war booty from France, which he briefly hesitated to claim in 1871 for that very reason, was Lorraine. In any case, after having done his preponderant share of putting the new Empire in jeopardy from the get-go through the annexation of Alsace–Lorraine, the grand master of *Realpolitik* relived his youthful courtship-and-casino

---

[11] Technically she was Isabella Loraine-Smith, but Bismarck ignored the "-Smith" (just as he dropped "-Schönhausen" from his own name): Palmer (1976): 12n.

[12] Palmer (1976): 11–13; Engelberg (1985): 144–47; Pflanze (1990): 44–46.

trauma preventively two-in-one. He guarded vicariously against that treacherous marriage and those catastrophic gambling losses both together when, as Imperial chancellor, he warded off a hostile foreign alliance by playing an alliance game in which he hedged all his bets, or counter-gambled.

The one major European nation that he enmeshed only indirectly in his tangled diplomatic web was the one he had been traumatically set to marry into and failed: his fickle fiancée's native England. His courtship fiasco duly flickers through his explanation for that missing direct alliance: that there was simply no forming a "permanent union" with England given her inherent volatility.[13]

This is as far as my previously published presentation of Bismarck's case went. It stopped too short in that it left Bismarck's *cauchemar des alliances* looking like a successful imaginary prevention of his traumatic fiasco of 1837 instead of the full traumatic reliving that it actually was. Futile efforts to ward off the traumatic outcome, although missing from Lou Andreas-Salomé's pattern of reliving, dominated Bismarck's. So a mere briefest addendum to my brief analysis is needed to specify that, since only Bismarck himself could operate his system of preventive alliances, it was bound to collapse whenever he left office, as he well knew. William II hastened the inevitable. Hard upon succeeding to the imperial throne, he dismissed Bismarck in 1890 rather than let him renew the so-called Reinsurance Treaty with Russia as his strategy for isolating France required. Out of office, Bismarck retreated to his estate in Pomerania, whence he looked on in impotent rage as France promptly contracted an alliance with Russia. His devious reliving was complete.

What was devious about his reliving was the disconnect between the surface and the subsurface story lines of his *cauchemar des alliances* once its personal referents in 1837 have been recognized: young Bismarck behind the German Empire and, more trickily, Isabella Loraine behind France and England both, not to mention the dethroned Spanish queen and the contentious French province. Among the surface signifiers, dizzying reversals of 1837 abound. Bismarck's Germany did not seek to ally with hostile France or fickle England as young Bismarck had sought to ally with Isabella

---

[13]Dictated 15 December 1891 (*"kein ewiger Bund"*): Bismarck (1934): 563.

Loraine; on the contrary, it engaged with the other powers instead. It strained in vain to prevent France from contracting an alliance with a third party as young Bismarck had never thought to try preventing his flighty fiancée from doing—to his later regret? Unlike young Bismarck, mature Bismarck's Empire did not gamble, but hedged all its bets several times over. The key to uncrossing the crossed signals of this waking nightmare is that they were crossed just to throw the reliver himself off, the way in a nightmare proper they would have been crossed just to throw the dreamer off. However crisscross, they accord no less with what, from Lou's case as well as Bismarck's, appears to be the basic recipe for a reliving: that the key traumatic elements, relations, and events should come into it by proxy, whether right side up or topsy-turvy, and with the foregone traumatic conclusion pending all the way.

Bismarck's felt guilt over his traumatically hapless and ruinous play for Isabella Loraine, although unrecorded at the time,[14] surfaced later as guilt felt over the annexation of Lorraine. His reliving was impassioned even if it was not self-generated but instead was likely prompted by the names of the Spanish queen and the French province when these commanded his attention. While his reliving did not parallel Lou's in form, his having been a tortured and hers always a straight transcription of their respective traumas, his matched—and even topped—hers in dynamism. A public figure of uncanny force and finesse combined, Bismarck imposed his will on his new Empire and on Europe even while remaining an overgrown neurasthenic baby behind the scenes. More, whereas Lou in reliving simply reran Nietzsche's traumatic rift with her, Bismarck in reliving raised the traumatic stakes from a pretty heiress's hand to his new Empire's very survival. His fatalism over-equalled Lou's in the form of a sinking feeling that he was waging a losing struggle only to delay his Empire's dire day of reckoning. In that diplomatic delaying action he nonetheless set aside all scruples as he propounded and practised power politics pure: such was the very meaning of the *Realpolitik* that was his ideological legacy to Germany. A tireless, imperious

[14]In his native German, however, "guilt" was contained in the "debt" with which the affair left him (*Schuld* and *Schulden* respectively).

drive tinged with pessimism: this has begun to look like the most prominent indicator of traumatic reliving, the way a fever signals an infection.

My case records feature two comparable political performances that were likewise trauma-driven a half century later. In the driving trauma behind the first of the two (oh shameless pun), on 29 August 1935 a roadster with Leopold III, king of the Belgians, improperly at the wheel, his wife Queen Astrid beside him, and the royal chauffeur relegated to the rumble seat, veered off the road in broad daylight; Astrid, hurled against a tree, was killed outright while Leopold and the chauffeur escaped bodily injury. Just over a year later the monarch improperly back-seated his foreign minister and took control of Belgian foreign policy to steer a disaster course of strict neutrality between France and Germany, thereby preventing the French from extending their line of fixed defensive fortifications against Germany to cover Belgium's eastern frontier. In launching his neutrality policy, Leopold told the government and nation that the shock of mechanical violence from the expected German invasion would be deadly—indeed, "will" be deadly—but that Belgium would at least be blameless.[15] And to the German minister in Brussels he compared Belgium's course to that of a motorist who even in broad daylight is exposed to a surprise collision at any turn. "We are at the mercy of an accident," he declared, as if to advertise his traumatic enterprise.

Unlike Bismarck, who identified with his Empire in his traumatic replay, Leopold remained the king of the Belgians in his. Less literally, Leopold's realm stood for its beloved lost queen, and the foreign minister in his tow doubled for his chauffeur in the rumble seat. This figurative casting by Leopold, unlike that by Bismarck, was one-on-one. Further, unlike Bismarck's reliving, Leopold's was straight and simple. And Leopold's felt guilt was as pronounced as Bismarck's was discreet: when the German invasion came, Leopold surrendered as commander-in-chief after some lame resistance and pointedly constituted himself a prisoner—again unharmed, to be sure, and with his palace remaining his residence this time too. Glaring as were these differences in form between the two relivings,

[15]Binion (1981a): 32.

they appear to have been just that superficial, like differences in handwritings of the same message in the same language. Some likenesses between the two relivings look equally superficial, such as the transposition of a jilting and of a royal death respectively to the plane of international war and peace: the traumatized chancellor and the traumatized king simply relived within their own spheres of activity, which were political, as did Lou within her lettered realm and Pirandello within his theatrical compass. Likenesses between Bismarck's and Leopold's relivings that were not shared with Lou's (let alone Pirandello's) were *ipso facto* superficial as well, such as the vain effort to forestall the traumatic outcome—an effort gigantic in Bismarck's case, feeble in Leopold's, and invisible in Lou's. The features common to all three relivings were accordingly of a deeper cut. At that deeper cut, all three relivings were pursued as if out of some higher necessity, resignedly and gloomily, yet with a passion that swept other parties along, and with the merest modicum of inhibition or scrupling. Still more fundamentally, all three were pursued unawares.

The last individual traumatic reliving to be considered, that by Adolf Hitler, scores tops in each and all of the basics and not-so-basics thus far suggested. Only in its initial configuration was the trauma that Hitler relived exceptional, having been what Freud called "additive" when, in the 1890s, he took the "summation" of traumas over time to be the etiological rule for neuroses. Hitler's "additive" trauma came in two instalments: the first filled him with latent anguish and anger that were released with a vengeance in the second, whereupon the two fused for him as if into a single episode. The germinal first instalment—dated 1907, when Hitler was eighteen—was his mother's death in agony from breast cancer after he induced her Jewish doctor to pack toxic doses of iodoform gauze onto her post-operative wound day after day in the vain hope of a miracle cure; he paid the big terminal bill on Christmas Eve. His was no ordinary bereavement in 1907, even apart from the smell of iodoform left in his nostrils. His mother had conceived him as her replacement for her three previous children, all lost to a diphtheria epidemic shortly before. Even while anxiously nursing and coddling him, she relived that prior traumatic maternal experience in that she resumed childbearing only after exactly the same length of time out as that experience itself had lasted from the first conception to the third death.[16] Her over-mothering of him through his whole childhood and adolescence left him with a lifelong feeling of special election and protection on top of a break-proof tie to her. With her picture ever around his neck, he served zealously and fearlessly as a foot soldier in World War I, experiencing it in spirit and flesh as the life-and-death struggle of the "motherland" (his distinctive term for his adoptive fatherland).

In mid-October 1918, after Germany had already sued for an armistice, a burst of poison gas on the front in Flanders blinded Hitler temporarily even as it strained his sense of invulnerability. The smell and sting of it linked it for him to the fateful iodoform, and he fell into a delirium such that, unlike his comrades gassed along with him, he was shipped cross-country for special care. After some slow recovery, he relapsed into blindness and went into a deathly depression at the announcement of the armistice of 11 November. A consulting neurologist drew him out of both by telling him under hypnosis that all was not lost: he could regain his eyesight by force of will, and defeated Germany could then be restored with his help. Although no anti-Semite before then, he heard this hortatory pep talk in his trance as a summons from on high to revive the motherland undermined by the parasitic-cancerous, poisonous, profiteering Jew. Such was his basic take on the 1918 defeat all the way from his psycho ward to the Berlin bunker even if he did learn in due course to temper the maniacal Jew-baiting of his agitational beginnings in Munich politics. And his basic project, as he phrased it in his early raw rhetoric, was to "poison the poisoner", namely "the Jew" (in the singular: again his distinctive usage), whose original identity as his mother's doctor is unmistakable.

Hitler replayed his two-part trauma on a larger scale through three simple equivalences. Filial Hitler figured as political Hitler, his dying mother as the motherland, and her Jewish doctor, blamed for the cancer, the iodoform, and the big terminal bill, as the Jewish parasite, poisoner, and profiteer. To "poison the poisoner"—or, in another of Hitler's early formulations, to "fight one poison with another"—meant to remove the Jew, guilty of Germany's defeat, from the national body, as Hitler often graphically put it, and

---

[16]For her arithmetical precision, see: Binion (1976): 54–55.

thereby to restore Germany while also magically undoing the defeat by removing its cause. Deciphered, this was the toxic failed miracle cure for his mother's cancer now conjoined with his own gas poisoning likewise construed as the Jew's dirty work. The miracle cure duly failed once again: his removal of the Jews from Germany, and indeed from most of Europe, did not prevent a second—and worse—German defeat. In form, then, Hitler's reliving was straightforward. His unavowed guilt over the toxic iodoform intended to remove his mother's cancer showed through his cover-up of the gas chambers meant to remove Germany's cancer. He relived with an infectious, ruthless fanaticism that lent his public persona a downright demoniac power in stark contrast to his private insignificance. He saw his historic course as preordained and pursued it with an increasingly nihilistic bent for all his strenuous, futile efforts to ward off the fated finale. "With the assurance of a sleepwalker I go the way Providence is directing me," he declared, sleepwalking (or somnambulism) being then appropriately the clinical term for the trance-like state in which severely traumatized patients might relive their traumas unawares.[17] In all of this, the suggested hallmark of traumatic reliving—a tireless, imperious drive tinged with fatalism—was as conspicuous in Hitler's case as it could get.

This boost to my tentative generalizations about how trauma is relived was ground enough for me to save Hitler's for the last of my four specimen relivings by individuals. But I did so for another reason: because it offers an easy transition to traumatic reliving by groups. That is in fact why I pried into it in the first place long years ago. Even to the naked psychohistorical eye it was as obvious that Hitler was interacting with a trauma-driven mass public as that he was himself trauma-driven. To begin with, his personal, poisonous traumatic agenda was distinctively his own. Raging against "the Jew" garnered the beer-hall agitator only a small, rowdy regional following in and around Munich, and the later extermination of the Jews within Nazi Germany's reach was the Führer's covert operation and not the Germans' collective doing. Yet in the years between his beer halls and his gas chambers, Hitler united Germany behind

[17]Domarus (1965): I, 606: *"Ich gehe mit traumwandlerischer Sicherheit den Weg, den mich die Vorsehung gehen heisst"* (14 March 1936); cf. above, ch. 2, n. 63.

him in avid submission, transforming a nation torn every which way by bloody ideological strife in the aftermath of the war lost in 1918 into a huge, grimly comical cheering squad shouting "Heil Hitler!" in unison to a marching beat.

Clearly Hitler struck a resonant German chord beneath the level of ideology when, after a year in jail for a failed attempt to putsch his way to power, he ceased his reiterative ranting against the Jew and intoned a second refrain in its place. This second, sustained refrain hit home nationwide. While the rest of political Germany sought ways to escape the penalties of the lost war, he alone proposed to refight that lost war instead. Only such territorial expansion as the German military pursued in 1914–1918, he contended, could meet Germany's vital needs. No longer blaming the Jew for the lost war in this context, he blamed the old Imperial leadership for confronting England and America before first gaining control of the continent. He proposed accordingly to expand Germany by stages, and initially by land only, endorsing Britain's naval and maritime supremacy in return for Britain's conceding him a free hand on the continent. In the event Britain declined the trade-off and, backed by America, resisted German expansion even on the continent alone, so that Hitler's war duly wound up as a rough re-run of its predecessor except that this time it was fought to the bitter last. His fatal failure to bring Britain around was not only foreseeable, but he actually invited it: he advertised his scheme to refight World War I by stages, the intended second stage being a showdown with England from an aggrandized continental power base.

It was, then, to refight the unwinnable war of 1914–1918 that Germany fell in line behind Hitler, such having been his sole professed policy after his failed Putsch of November 1923 in Munich. He pushed that sole professed policy insistently right and left for some years before he muffled it for foreign ears as of late 1930, when his following had swelled gigantically. The indication is that through his projected replay of the lost war of 1914–1918 he spoke to a national trauma wrought by the 1918 defeat. In no way did the terms of his proposed replay of that lost war bear on his two-part personal trauma. At the same time, because his breakdown of late 1918 accompanied Germany's, he was singularly sensitive to the traumatic national impact of the military defeat. In his Bavarian political beginnings he took the pulse of his fevered public even while dumping on the

Jew: the result was that programme for refighting the lost war that was his single pitch for power once he refounded his party nationally in January 1925. But above all, the facts of the 1918 defeat themselves point straight to a national trauma. For that defeat came as a frightful shock to an incredulous nation fed on victory bulletins to the last in 1918 as its armies overran the remnants of the Russian Empire on the one side and, on the other, launched two successive final offensives against Paris from bases deep in enemy territory in Flanders. Then at summer's end, without forewarning, the High Command declared a bust for want of sufficient manpower reserves. Panic and pandemonium, regional revolutions and fierce scrambles for power, swept Germany in the short run. The long run was Hitlerism: Germany's traumatically lost war of 1914–1918 relived.

Seen under the methodologist's searchlight, collective trauma and reliving are baffling. A group traumatized apart from the individuals composing it, preserving the memory of that trauma independently of its members' individual memories, then reliving that trauma through its unsuspecting members: all this is dauntingly hard to conceive. An individual trauma relived unawares is conceptual trouble enough, but at least there is a tangible individual cervical container for the traumatic memory being relived. Does that individual cervical container also harbour collective memories dispersed a hundred-, a thousand-, or a million-fold? If so, how are those collective memories transmitted down the generations? And how are they acquired by newcomers to the traumatized group from the outside? These unfathomables would have tempted me to write off group reliving as a will-o'-the-wisp except for two hard facts. One is that groups do manifestly act on their own to collective ends distinct from their members' individual interests, aims, or motives. I wrote a whole book to show group process at work in diverse historical modes and spheres,[18] and thus on this point I now claim the weary scholar's privilege of mere affirmation. The other hard fact is that history provides a panoply of group doings that reconfigure earlier experiences by the same group with all the earmarks of individual traumas writ large. Up to a point, such reliving by groups can be seen as parallel individual relivings within groups, especially within small groups

[18] Binion (2005b).

having undergone no significant turnover in membership. The larger the group and the greater its turnover of members, however, the more implausible such an alternative line of explanation becomes. I propose accordingly to accept the fact of group reliving, to ignore its elusive mechanics, and to review a few sample instances in comparison with the individual patterns so far uncovered. For this cavalier procedure I boast high scientific sanction: the invariable speed at which light reaches an observer moving either toward or away from its source is likewise unquestionable and unimaginable both at once, yet it keeps our cosmos on an even keel.[19]

The replay of Germany's 1918 trauma of defeat, to start there, was prompted by Hitler's pitch to lead the way. Its form was as elementary and as nearly literal as circumstances permitted: a second thrust for continental dominion, this one launched by overt design, which turned into an unwanted, unwinnable second world war, the German defeat being this time driven home conclusively. The guilt imputed to Germany for the outbreak and conduct of the first war was as if confirmed many times over in its re-run under Hitler. To relaunch the lost war from a territorial, economic, and military power base drastically reduced by the 1918 defeat took a titanic, ruthless purposiveness of a traumatic cut—a force of will such as was enjoined on traumatized Hitler hypnotically in 1918 and by him in turn on the traumatized German people as they fell in behind him. Hitler had clinched the national reliving by the start of 1942, when, as he put it, fate had decreed that Germany should find itself facing the same enemies as the last time round.[20] By then a fatalistic mood had already set in nationwide despite the initial victories of German diplomacy and arms—a mood that, with due traumatic illogic, did not impede Germany's continuing struggle to the bitter end. The traumatized German public felt itself in the grip of a historical imperative that even its mighty Führer could not master. It was replaying by deputation, but also replaying along. And it was

---

[19]Comparably, gravitation has been an accepted fact since Newton, but its transmission remains a mystery. Or in an analogue closer to home, Freud was fond of rebutting rational arguments against the unconscious by quoting Charcot: "*Cela n'empêche pas d'exister.*"

[20]Binion (1976): 107 and n. 134 (15 February 1942). Italy was shortly to switch sides, clinching the replay in Europe.

replaying with a full run of the features characteristic of individual replays—guilt, titanic will, and fatalism foremost.

On next to a mass trauma relived episodically in fact and chronically in fancy, to wit, the trauma that Europeans were at one in suffering as the initially exhilarating Revolution of 1789 in France gradually degenerated into mob violence and official terror. Slowly but surely the promise of human self-emancipation miscarried, the dream of reason bred monsters, the light from heaven turned infernal, the glorious dawn yielded to blackest night: such in countless variants was the rhetoric and imagery thrown up by the event from one end of Europe to the other. Europeans all felt the shock earlier or later, in anger or sorrow, in distress or denial. That shock was, as Shelley put it, "the master theme of the epoch in which we live".[21]

It issued in the cultural revolt against the old order, Romanticism, which dominated Europe for a half century. Sky-high hopes of Kingdom Come shot to hell: this traumatic sequence shows through the Romantics' entire thematic repertoire. The antithesis between the ideal and the real, the mutual affinity of the sublime and the grotesque, the conflicted impulse to reform and to flee the world, the stock Romantic genres of the fairy tale and the horror story, the Romantics' collapsed hierarchies of style and subject matter in the arts, their signature motif of lost illusions or, more graphically still, of a celestial vision turning (or turning out to be) spectral: indeed, the full run of Romantic staples bore the impress of their historic referent of 1789–1794. Meanwhile in Romantic Europe the failed Revolution itself was refought sporadically, off paper and off canvas, in loose concurrence across the continent in 1830 beginning in France, and in climactic unison from city to city in 1848 again beginning in France, with the values and slogans of 1789 everywhere hoisted high, and with the revolutionaries all heroically prepared for the worst in their hearts of hearts. The new revolutionaries came off least ill in France itself, which isn't saying much: there they at least achieved a change of dynasty in 1830, then a republic in 1848—one which, however, succumbed to an imperial coup d'état by Napoleon's nephew in imitation of the avuncular precedent that had sealed the first, revolutionary republic's fate. As Karl Marx quipped, history was replayed as farce.

[21]Shelley to Byron, 8 September 1816, in Byron (1922), 25.

The traumatic wreck of the revolutionary hope after 1789 was not pinpointed in time, nor did it come through to all Europeans simultaneously. Whereas the 1918 defeat struck the Germans all at once, the Europeans' passage from thrill to shudder after the fall of the Bastille was piecemeal and cumulative. Yet millions of individual reactions could hardly have run to type, each reflecting the French revolutionary events in the same guises and disguises to form a cultural movement all of a piece. Rather, the traumatic shock effect spread among Europeans as the event unfolded, being eventually felt by them in sync and relived in sync. Whereas this person-by-person build-up of the trauma of the Revolution-run-amuck has no counterpart in individual experience, the subsequent two-track figurative and physical reliving of the trauma of the failed Revolution very much has one: witness Lou's or Pirandello's reliving in both fiction and fact. In the realm of ideas and ideals, further, the Romantics' cult of energy and premium on passion, their celebration of heroism over moralism, their fascination with human evil, their dramas and philosophies of fate: all resonate with the unscrupulous, often guilt-tinged drive that actuates individual reliving together with a companion feeling of being driven.

The worst mass trauma on record was likewise all-European, and it too spread like a contagion throughout Europe. In fact it was a contagion, the Black Death, and its traumatic legacy included Europe itself as a felt identity rather than just a geographic entity. More, that trauma too was relived both literally and figuratively, and at the same time both episodically and chronically—literally and episodically through repeated local recurrences of the pestilence, figuratively and chronically through popular cultural artifacts that haunted plagued Europe for over two centuries without letup, most notably the Dance of the Dead. This chronic cultural reliving was the more tenacious of the two. The literal, episodic recurrences tapered off irregularly, ending in 1772 just where the initial pandemic had ended, in the area of Moscow. But then the culture of death spawned by the trauma, after having ducked out of the age of classicism and enlightenment, resurfaced on a grand scale beginning punctually in the mid-1770s with all its macabre motifs sexed up and juggled around.[22]

[22]On this whole theme, see: Binion (2004): 119–35.

Guilt dominated the first and deadliest wave of the pestilence, the Black Death proper of 1347–1352, which wiped out about half the population of Europe. When it struck, it was seen on all sides as a divine punishment for human iniquity. In the Dance of the Dead, figures of death danced off every last soul indiscriminately and mercilessly to hell. Here in a nutshell were the guilt, the escalation, the compellingness, the ruthlessness, and the fatalism that come close to being earmarks of traumatic reliving, and at that with no overt reference in the Dance to the plague itself: as against its identical literal reliving as the plague recurrent, its symbolic reliving, though transparent, went unsuspected by its participants. (Only the monk John Lydgate did allude once to the plague in his free English translation of the Dance from the wall of the *Cimetière des Innocents*). A further near-staple of episodic reliving, the futile effort to stave off the dire traumatic outcome, was more developed in a late spinoff of the Dance of the Dead, Death and the Maiden, in which a maiden's plea for death to spare her goes brutally unheard: the victims were danced off to damnation more resignedly in the Dance of the Dead itself. So, like the traumatic plunge from the Rights of Man to the wrongs of men in revolutionary France, the massive mass trauma of the Black Death was relived culturally in the same format as individual traumas, and with the same bluntness and subtlety intermixed.

Or have I been tending to twist my historic cases so as to squeeze them all into a common mold? Distinctive formal features shared by some are lacking in others. My first exhibit in kind, Lou Andreas-Salomé's reliving, turns out not to have run to type with the others in full: her guilt pangs over her trauma, if any, were inconspicuous, nor in reliving it did she either heighten or resist its fated finale. Comparably on the collective side, Europeans neither scrapped any scruples nor gained any striking new powers in order to relive the Black Death in kind or later to re-experience Romantically their traumatic comedown from their glorious high of 1789. Would such features of traumatic reliving be typical but not universal? Perhaps—although another group reliving on a vast scale that I have probed, that of Christendom's self-inflicted trauma of the Death of God,[23] is to my knowledge unique in almost every particular. Among other

---

[23] Binion (1986) and Binion (1993).

peculiarities, it has been relived in segments, the lapsed articles of faith reviving and relapsing singly in new forms. The traumatic pattern is nonetheless unmistakable segment by segment. What pattern? Again tentatively put, that of individuals or groups unsuspectingly reconfiguring and reactivating the key elements of a previous overwhelming experience. Its usual outer features—the guilt, the radical empowerment, the escalation, the fatalism, the losing attempt to forestall or undo the outcome—would be just that: usual rather than typical. Any estimate of how usual they are will take far more case studies than I alone have been able to conduct.

So far I have drawn exclusively on my own studies of traumatic reliving in history not only because I know them best, but also because I know of so few others. Of these others, a trenchant case history of the chronic form of reliving is Frank Graziano's reconstruction of how grown-up Rose of Lima reconfigured her diverse childhood sufferings in a ritual of saintly self-torment.[24] The oldest full-fledged study of episodic reliving that I know whether individual or collective (not counting Freud's speculative Moses book[25]) is Joel Markowitz's exacting account of how a traumatic massacre at Courtrai in 1302 of Norman armoured horsemen charging Welsh foot soldiers head-on was relived repeatedly by their horse-borne Norman successors with mounting penalties for over a century, and then how, with the obsolescence of heavy armour, this suicidal tactical routine, rather than die out, went into remission until it revived within the entire French military beginning with the wars of the Revolution and Napoleon.[26] Only on the single key point of the spread of a traumatic effect well beyond its original host, and after three-and-a-half centuries of latency at that, do Markowitz's findings outrun mine on group trauma relived episodically.

The most far-reaching historic studies of episodic traumatic reliving that I know are Jay Y. Gonen's of Jewish history.[27] According to Gonen, Jewish history is replete with traumas and suffused with the compulsion to relive them. Furthermore, historic time is compressed in the Jewish perception to the effect that new traumas are aligned

---

[24] Graziano (2004): 157–64.
[25] See above, ch. 2, n. 72.
[26] Markowitz (1969): 115–70.
[27] Gonen (1975); Gonen (1979); Gonen (2005).

with old ones, real and mythic alike. "In messianic time," Gonen explains, "past and future are fused into an eternal present where all traumas meet and repeat."[28] Thus Israelis instinctively assimilated the traumatic surprise attack and initial success of the Arab armies in the Yom Kippur War of 1973 to the destruction of the First Temple and again of the Second Temple a couple of thousand years before; as they saw it, a Third Temple was accordingly on the line in 1973. In another such Jewish traumatic conflation, Samson's dying defiance of the Philistines prefigured the choice of suicide over surrender in 73 A.D. by the defenders of Masada, the last stronghold of the Jewish revolt against the Romans, and Masada in turn linked up with the heroic Warsaw Ghetto uprising. Following the victorious Six Days War of 1967 the Israeli army ritualized the celebration of this Masada complex in order to redeem those three defeats and infuse them with heroism. Nor was that all. Those three Jewish defeats in turn rejoined a whole string of others out of ancient lore and modern history alike: the bondage in Egypt, the subjugation by Assyria, Babylonia, and Rome, the expulsion from Spain, and finally the Holocaust. With the Holocaust, however, the measure was full. The Jews were left vowing: Never again! "It was a vow to turn any prospective repetition of trauma into a mastery of the trauma," Gonen writes. "At the same time it was a prospective wish converted into a retrospective affirmation."[29] In an arresting overview Gonen adds: "The rules of Jewish history set by Yahweh condition Jewish expectations from history. The most basic rule is that destruction always precedes rebuilding until traumatic repetition will finally be overcome or mastered at the End of Days—i.e., never."[30] The sorry upshot is a delusional tendency to pursue redemption by courting traumas in hopes of mastering them. "The traumas will be relived while the hoped-for mastery will still be deferred to the End of Days. He who lives in a messianic time compression is doomed to perpetual traumatic replay."[31] Gonen's grasp of traumatic reliving exceeds my own in that it encompasses, together with the temporal, historic realm, the timeless, mythic realm in which, as Yahweh's people know, all

---

[28] Gonen to me, 26 February 2006.
[29] Gonen to me, 26 February 2006.
[30] Gonen to me, 26 February 2006.
[31] Gonen to me, 26 February 2006.

traumatic reliving takes place. Their traumatic culture is distinctive, however, insofar as they do not so much contrive to relive their old traumas as construe their new ones as relivings of the old.

Markowitz's and Gonen's historic studies of episodic traumatic reliving, even as they broaden the scope of mine, attest to the need for diverse additional contributions of the kind before firm generalizing can begin. Hoping to highlight this need while also helping to meet it, I offer next a new empirical study of my own that compelled me to correct some of my prior misconceptions about collective traumatic reliving in particular.

CHAPTER FOUR

Reliving in history: A closeup

It is high time for a fresh, close look at another historic group trauma relived. I propose to take such a look at the collapse of the Third French Republic as re-enacted through the collapse of the Fourth.[1] Besides adding to my pool of traumatic relivings, this new enquiry will display my mode of analysis in hopes of facilitating other enquiries into the phenomenon of traumatic reliving at its most baffling: *en groupe*. Or should I have written more positively: "at its most challenging"? After all, human history is what people have done or experienced, no more and no less, and what they have done or experienced in groups predominates. Hence this recurrent, pervasive mode of group action, traumatic reliving, cries out for the historian's attention.

The Third French Republic came to an inglorious end between Bordeaux on 16 June and Vichy on 10 July 1940. That 16 June in Bordeaux, makeshift capital of France at the height of the German invasion, Premier Paul Reynaud made way for a successor, Marshal

[1]This chapter is adapted from my "De Gaulle as Pétain", *Clio's Psyche*, XII, No. 2 (September 2005), 37, 56–66, with fourteen historians' comments 66–97 and my replies 97–100.

Philippe Pétain, to request armistice terms. Then on that 10 July as much of the French parliament as could meet in the watering town of Vichy voted Pétain's government full powers to draft a new, authoritarian constitution for popular approval and to rule by fiat meanwhile. Some eighteen years later, between 28 May and 1–3 June 1958, the Fourth French Republic came to an equally inglorious end. In Paris on that 28 May Premier Pierre Pflimlin made way for General Charles de Gaulle to succeed him in order to avert a coup d'état by the military fearful of a sellout to rebels fighting French rule in Algeria. Then on that 1–3 June the parliament in Paris voted a government under de Gaulle full power to draft a new, authoritarian constitution for popular approval and to rule by fiat meanwhile. Like Pétain, further, de Gaulle was to work on the new constitution through a consultative council and to legislate through the Conseil d'État. Unlike 1940, on the other hand, the chambres voted separately in 1958, and de Gaulle's special powers were limited to six months. Also, Pétain did not, whereas de Gaulle did, deliver on a new constitution for popular approval, but never mind: for now I am considering only how the two republics fell.

Regime change has been the rule in modern France after any major military defeat like the one that brought Pétain to power in 1940. On the other hand, a mandate for regime change as a condition for taking power was unprecedented when de Gaulle demanded one in 1958. In seeking regime change, de Gaulle was manifestly out to rectify his failure to overhaul France's political institutions and political culture to his liking at the Liberation, when he had pushed in vain for a strong, independent executive for the nascent Fourth Republic. At the same time, the mandate he sought in 1958 for regime change and, meanwhile, personal rule threw back, in letter and spirit both, to the one granted to his deadly rival of World War II, Marshal Pétain, on 10 July 1940. On taking power in 1940, Pétain had grandiloquently made—in his own famous words—"the gift of my person to France". In much the same vein, de Gaulle, when bucking for power in 1958, styled himself a loner at his country's disposal "who belongs to no one and to everyone".[2] Like Pétain before him, de Gaulle aspired to

---

[2]Pétain, 16 June 1940; de Gaulle, 19 May, 1958. The Pétainist journal *Rivarol* coupled these two quotations to justify supporting de Gaulle out of fidelity to Pétain: Rousso (1987): 90.

represent eternal France as against any special or passing interests within the body politic. For his return in 1958 he proudly insisted on being excused from appearing in person before the National Assembly as its rules required. To stand aloof in that way accorded with his mystique, to be sure, but it accorded as well with Pétain's failure to appear in person before the parliament on 10 July 1940 in Vichy. After much wrangling, de Gaulle settled on reading a brief statement of intent to the Chambre in Paris on 1 June 1958 and stalking off before the debate on his investiture. Then, after having been voted in with the emergency powers he demanded, he presided mutely the next day over the debate on his constituent mandate.

The replay by de Gaulle in 1958 of Pétain in 1940 was only the more faithful for one big tactical difference. Pétain in 1940 did not put in for a regime change until after he had succeeded Reynaud for a different purpose: to negotiate an armistice rather than continue the losing war outside of metropolitan France. De Gaulle too was given power in 1958 for a purpose other than regime change: to resolve the raging Algerian crisis. He, however, declined to address the Algerian issue directly in his cryptic public pronouncements before his empowerment. Indeed, he proposed no specifics of any kind other than regime change on the contrived ground that France's troubles, Algeria inclusive, were all attributable to the nature of the political regime in place. He evaded the Algerian issue, moreover, in terms exactly applicable to June 1940 when on 15 May 1958 he broke a three-year public silence to blame "the degradation of the State" for "our army's troubles in combat, our national dislocation, our loss of independence".[3] In effect, with seditious generals in Algeria clamouring for his return and poised to invade the mainland otherwise, he struck a tacit bargain with the Assembly: he would return only in exchange for a constituent mandate like the one granted to Pétain in 1940. Tactics aside, the basic equivalence of 1958 with 1940 remains: just as Pétain had used the 1940 defeat to destroy the Third Republic,[4] so did de Gaulle use the 1958 Algerian crisis to destroy the Fourth Republic.

---

[3]*"... le trouble de l'armée au combat, la dislocation nationale, la perte de l'indépendance"*. As for *"la dégradation de l'État"*, "State" in this context had a distinctly Pétainist resonance, Pétain having ruled in the name of "the French State" rather than of the French Republic.

[4]This was Henri Queuille's formulation, quoted by Noguères (1955): 118. Léon Blum went further: see République Française, Haute Cour de Justice (1945): 79.

But de Gaulle did not destroy the Fourth Republic without its help any more than Pétain destroyed the Third Republic without its help. So our focus must now broaden from just those two historic personages to the fall of the Third and of the Fourth Republics compared—to the structural overlap between those two events and ultimately to the psychohistorical meaning of that overlap. When I say "structural overlap" I am thinking far afield: of Claude Lévi-Strauss's structural anthropology with its "permutation groups", or clusters of key elements of a myth that exists in various forms. Those key elements à la Lévi-Strauss all occur in every version of such a myth. Some occur literally, others topsy-turvy as when, say, a sterile old maid in one variant is a pregnant young boy in another. Lévi-Strauss tended to identify the key elements of a myth circularly as just those elements that he found repeated in every version of the myth, but *passons*: genius has its privileges.

Seen in this comparative perspective, the key elements of the two non-mythic events of June–July 1940 and May–June 1958, the fall of the Third and the fall of the Fourth French Republic, match up for the most part quite closely right on the surface. Each of the two events was a high French political drama played out during an acute national crisis. In each an incumbent chief of government, without being voted down, stepped aside for a successor from outside the regular political ranks. Both times the heads of the two chambres resisted until the president of the republic overrode them. Each of the two outside successors was a military figure with a mythic aureole as France's saviour in an hour of dire need—Pétain as the hero of Verdun, which he had defended tenaciously and victoriously in 1916 against an all-out German offensive, and de Gaulle as "the man of June 18" (1940), when from London he had called on his compatriots to join him in resisting the German occupation despite the armistice announced by Pétain the day before. Each was a staunch traditionalist and a passionate patriot besides. The parties for their part split over the two comeback saviours each in turn. Fittingly, the two were themselves both down on parties and high instead on strong personal rule in direct rapport with the nation. To quote the expert opinion of Robert Paxton: "De Gaulle and his former mentor and adversary resembled each other in many respects, but in none so clearly as when they talked contemptuously of the 'regime of parties'."[5] The parties split over the crisis issue itself as well, which, moreover, was the same at bottom in 1958 as in 1940: whether to negotiate with the enemy, German and Algerian respectively. In May 1958 as in June 1940, finally, the government came under severe pressure from its own military, although to exactly the opposite effect in 1958, when the army nixed all negotiations, as against 1940, when Marshal Pétain, Commander-in-Chief Maxime Weygand, and Admiral François Darlan had all demanded negotiations. But again: in permutation groups, diametric opposites meet.

The parliamentarians for their part yielded to Pétain and again to de Gaulle only under outside pressure acutely felt, although the sources of that outside pressure differed superficially from 1940 to 1958. Those deputies and senators who met in the Vichy casino in July 1940 to bury the Third Republic were nervously mindful of the German army fifty kilometres off in Moulins, of a fresh French division under Pétain's confederate Weygand, now minister of national defence, in nearby Clermont-Ferrand, and in Vichy itself of bands of collaborationist thugs behind Jacques Doriot.[6] "What was at work was fear," Léon Blum later testified.[7] At work too then in Vichy was Pierre Laval, who later concurred: "I saw fear break out."[8] On the other hand, the outside pressure felt in parliament in June 1958 came from a single source, the French army, but likewise from several directions—from Algeria primarily, although also from Corsica (seized by parachutists on 24 May 1958 on orders from Algiers), from Germany, and from suspected points within France proper, besides enjoying police sympathy in Paris itself. Beginning on 13 May 1958, when a self-styled committee of public safety led by generals and colonials ("*pieds noirs*") seized power in Algiers and pugnaciously put Paris on notice, political leaders from President René Coty and premier Pflimlin on down, and not least de Gaulle himself, invoked the imminence of civil war again and again. An ultimatum from Algiers early on 29 May

[5]Paxton (1972): 351.

[6]See especially Garçon (1946): 153–54; République Française, Haute Cour de Justice (1945): 48, 77–80; cf. ibid., 141 (Maxime Weygand).

[7]*Procès Pétain*, 77.

[8]*Procès Laval*, 153.

forced de Gaulle's appointment, and when a mute de Gaulle met with the National Assembly that 1 June, "Operation Resurrection" (as the Army called its projected coup) was all set to go, the capital being already invested by paratroopers in civilian dress. "I cannot concur in a vote given under pressure of an insurrection and threat of military force," Pierre Mendès France memorably told a mute de Gaulle from the floor of the Chambre, adding: "the decision the Assembly is about to take, as everyone here knows, is no free decision."[9]

More, in June–July 1940 as later in May–June 1958 the political leadership of France was largely demoralized. In 1940 it was reeling from a current, crushing military defeat. In 1958 it was shot through with a sense of ineluctable decline given the loss of Indochina in 1954, then of Morocco and Tunisia two years later. Deep down it felt, rightly, that France could not hold Algeria much longer, being ideologically on the wrong side of the war of repression there. True parity for eight million natives with the million European colonists in Algeria was in fact the last thing the French really wanted—and, fortunately for them, the last thing that the rebels wanted either, as it could only slow their struggle for independence. (That most Algerians probably would have preferred true parity to independence is sadly beside the point.) Hence little by little, as they continued pledging to keep Algeria French, successive French governments lost faith with all concerned, including themselves. No less demoralizing for the political assemblies confronted with a constitutional challenge in 1940 and again in 1958 was the discredit into which they had fallen by then among the broad public: Pétain and later de Gaulle were hardly crying in the wilderness against (as the phrase then ran) the omnipotent, impotent chambres.

For all these outer and inner pressures on them, the parliamentarians committed regime suicide both times only irresolutely, with split votes and divided wills.[10] On this key score too the specifics, but not

---

[9]Pierre Mendès France, in *Journal officiel: Débats parlementaires, Assemblée Nationale,* 1 June 1958: 2577. Mendès's intervention recalled Léon Blum's argument for the illegitimacy of the vote on 10 July 1940: "Our mandate forbids us to yield to force": Winock (1968): 299.

[10]The National Assembly's vote of 329 to 224 with 39 abstentions on 1 June 1958 was much closer than the parliamentary vote of 569 to 80 with 17 abstentions on 10 July 1940, but less so if, for 1940, the seventy-odd Communists disqualified since 1939 and the thirty parliamentarians detained in North Africa are counted as opposed.

the fundamentals, differed between the fall of the Third and the fall of the Fourth Republic. And the "permutations" between the two were all transparent, despite even so drastic a surface contrast as the one between the top brass pressing for negotiations with the enemy in the one case and pressing against negotiations with the enemy in the other, or again between the two gigantic successor figures of Pétain and de Gaulle. Pétain's credentials as saviour were unique in 1940, as were de Gaulle's in 1958: hence in that crucial regard they were two of a kind however much it hurt some former maréchalistes to vote for de Gaulle in 1958 and some gaullistes of the first hour to vote against him then.

This issue of remembering 1940 in 1958 requires us to leave the timeless mythic realm of "permutation groups" *à la* Lévi-Strauss for the historic realm to which my material properly belongs. Unlike myths, which need to have emerged in no known sequence, the Third and the Fourth French Republics fell by turns, in 1940 and 1958 respectively. Hence the 1958 fall, in its structural equivalence to the 1940 fall, was a re-edition of it, a replay. The actors in that second regime change were re-enacting the first regime change beneath the surface—or, to call a spade a spade, unconsciously. There are several possible circumstances in which people re-enact, or relive, events unconsciously, but the most usual is unmistakably the one on display on this occasion: when the event being relived was traumatic.

That the fall of France in 1940 was traumatic for the French requires, I hope, no elaborate evidencing. Robert Paxton, to cite him alone, begins his authoritative history of Vichy France: "No one who lived through the French debacle of May–June 1940 ever quite got over the shock." And he adds, crossing his t's diagnostically: "For Frenchmen, confident of a special role in the world, the six weeks' defeat by German armies was a shattering trauma."[11] The surface effect of that trauma was a widespread public apathy or lethargy, a sort of collective numbing, that endured at least as long as the Vichy regime itself and that was to help shroud the Vichy experience in selective amnesia afterwards.[12] Something of that detachment reappeared to

[11] Paxton (1972): 3. Similarly for Lacouture (1984): 449, the French public under Vichy was "a traumatized mass". Further, Jackson (2003): 2 ("the trauma of the defeat of 1940"—and, quoting René Rémond, "a deep and lasting traumatism") and passim.
[12] Paxton (1972): 237. In loose French usage, the Occupation is often called "traumatic": see, for example, Rousso (1987): 83.

impress outside observers during the crisis of May 1958, when, even with the National Assembly surrounded by tanks to protect it from an expected assault on the capital by the rebellious French army, the population at large looked on as at a staged spectacle of *son et lumière* or else blithely went off holidaying for the Pentecost weekend.[13]

This popular disconnect from the traumatic reliving underway on the governmental and parliamentary levels highlights the peculiarity that, whereas all of France was traumatized in June–July 1940, all of France relived that trauma only by proxy in May–June 1958, through its political representation, which it no longer even felt to be quite representative of it at that. Or rather, the political establishment of the Fourth Republic alone relived the fall of the Third; the rest of France remained outside the charmed, or accursed, circle of power brokerage. The big exception that proved the rule of public exclusion and self-exclusion in 1958 was a massive march in Paris on 28 May from the Place de la Nation to the Place de la République in support of the existing regime against the threat from the Algerian junta and from de Gaulle alike: it changed precisely nothing. De Gaulle merely postponed his sneak entry into Paris by some hours; for the rest, the scenario ran its prescribed course. A republican militant recollected: "Our illusions lasted a single evening behind the placards and banners. While the crowd was swarming, the dénouement was being prepared behind the scenes: the soldier's grand entry."[14] It cannot be said even loosely that France as a whole got itself into the same political mess or its equivalent in 1958 as in 1940. Only on the parliamentary level was the menacing pressure from the outside comparable between 10 July 1940 and the first days of June 1958. The Germans in Moulins, Weygand in Clermont, and Doriot in Vichy in 1940, then in 1958 the seditious generals and riotous colonists: all remained at a distinct existential remove from the bulk of the French public.

If, then, the French people collectively did not contrive in 1958 to relive their 1940 trauma of defeat, who did? An obvious suspect is the prime beneficiary of that reliving, *le grand Charles*. He did buck for, and get, the Pétain role in the replay. He did hoist the Algerian crisis into a regime crisis 1940-style as the replay required. The putschists

[13]Pentecost fell on Sunday, 25 May.

[14]Winock (1978): 206; more generally on the public's sense of exclusion, 198–218.

rallied to him because he had defied a capitulationist government in 1940, and the antiputschists yielded to him because he had restored republican legitimacy in 1944. For all that, he did not himself conjure up the political crisis that enabled the replay of 10 July 1940; rather, he hijacked that political crisis and replay for his own public and private purposes. One public purpose was the obvious one of making good his failure of 1944–1946 to forge a new regime in his own image as Pétain had done just previously. At the same time he too, along with his compatriots, would seem to have been traumatized by the debacle of May–June 1940, although in his case with a personal twist. Appointed undersecretary of war in Reynaud's cabinet on 5 June, he failed in his first assigned task of winning British air support for France. Then his colleagues pooh-poohed him for planning a Breton redoubt. Finally, from London on 16 June he and Churchill together telephoned Reynaud in Bordeaux with a British offer to fuse the French and British nationalities until victory, whereupon he flew to Bordeaux in high hopes, only to learn that the offer had fallen flat and Reynaud had resigned. This last and worst setback resurfaced in thin disguise in June 1958 when, fast upon his empowerment, he flew to Algiers to proclaim a fusion of the French and Algerian nationalities: it too duly fell flat.[15] Meanwhile, from Bordeaux on 17 June 1940 he flew back to London as if in a daze[16] and there that evening learned of Pétain's bid for an armistice and order to cease combat. His dominant reaction was denial, indeed double denial. He denied the military defeat and denied the legitimacy of Pétain's defeatist regime both at once. (Unlike the former, the latter denial was only implicit in his early public pronouncements, as in his allusion over the BBC on 3 August 1940 to "the so-called government formed in the panic of Bordeaux"[17]; in private, however, he denounced Pétain's "treason" promptly on 17 June.[18]) His historic identity was built on that double denial of the national trauma of 1940.

---

[15] "I declare that as of today France considers that in all of Algeria there ... are only full-fledged Frenchmen [*à part entière*]": *Le Monde*, 6 June (1958): 3.

[16] Lacouture (1984): 363 compares him to a sleepwalker.

[17] Unlike the first, the second denial was only implicit in his early public pronouncements, as in his allusion over the BBC on 3 August 1940 to "the so-called government formed in the panic of Bordeaux". Lacouture (1984): 348. But in private he denounced Pétain's "treason" promptly on 17 June: Lacouture (1984): 367.

[18] Lacouture (1984): 367.

With that historic identity went a powerful ambivalence toward Pétain. Its positive side, which enabled de Gaulle to assume the Pétain role in 1958, may have poked out of hiding already in December 1946, when he reportedly told a confidant: "France needed both Marshal Pétain and General de Gaulle in June 1940."[19] Even while playing the Pétain role in 1958 he appeared rather to be enacting the historic personage de Gaulle. Where Pétain had aggrandized himself on taking power ("*Nous, Philippe Pétain* ...") in the belief that a "providential mission was reserved for him",[20] de Gaulle, who acquired that same belief in turn, characteristically spoke of his public persona in the third person (de Gaulle this, de Gaulle that), as if to advertise that he was role-playing. On 19 May 1958, in his first public pitch to return to power, he told the press that the French instinctively cried "*Vive de Gaulle*!" whenever they were carried away by anguish or hope: such was his wishful thinking of himself as the national idol that Pétain had in fact been in June–July 1940. Pétain scored highest in his triumphal beginnings in Bordeaux and Vichy. If the parliament on 10 July 1940 invested him with more power than any sovereign of France ever enjoyed,[21] the populace was far from dissenting. "He was a sort of life raft to which all hands reached out," the leader of the Senate later testified.[22] Or as Laval put it: "More than a king, more than an emperor, he symbolized, he incarnated, France."[23] Such a personification of France was de Gaulle's ambition for himself in turn after his paltry start in London on 18 June 1940 and his long, slow struggle for a following in Pétain's France. In 1958, much of the impressive near-80% popular vote for his new constitution on 28 September was a climactic endorsement of his comeback itself, yet it still fell far short, by all estimates, of the untabulated Pétainolatry of June–July 1940. As a postscript to his imitation of Pétain, after having been returned to power in 1958 by the putschists because of his legendary refusal of a negotiated surrender to the German enemy in 1940, he wound up negotiating a surrender to the Algerian enemy after all in 1961.

---

[19] Rousso (1987): 43–44; further, ibid., 43–50.
[20] Szaluta (1980): 439.
[21] Lacouture (1984): 411.
[22] Lacouture (1984).
[23] Garçon (1946): 165.

Not just de Gaulle's historic identity dating from 18 June 1940, but his entire earlier career, was dominated by intense ambivalence toward Pétain, his first regimental commander in 1912–1913 and his loyal patron of the 1920s and 1930s.[24] That ambivalence exploded fatefully over a history of the French soldier that de Gaulle ghostwrote to order for Pétain in 1925–1927. In ghostwriting for Pétain he was already playing at being Pétain even while impressing his own personality on the commandeered historical work. In 1928, however, Pétain assigned another hand to revise the chapter on the First World War, thereby shattering de Gaulle's fond fancy that the book was his by common consent even if Pétain meant to sign off on it. De Gaulle did not simply boil over; he demanded open acknowledgement of his authorship up front in the published volume, telling Pétain boldly and baldly that "others will perforce discover it later" anyhow.[25] Pétain filed the manuscript away. De Gaulle on his side kept a copy and in 1938 contracted to publish it without Pétain's few, pedestrian rewordings. Pétain, consulted tardily and dryly, objected sharply, telling his erstwhile protégé: "Your attitude is very painful to me."[26] Shifting his stance, de Gaulle appealed against Pétain's objection in conciliatory, ingratiating accents, stressing his distinctive and ambitious personal investment of ideas and style. Pétain relented, only to take keen offence next when de Gaulle refused to let him check the proofs as agreed, and again especially when de Gaulle rephrased a co-authored dedication acknowledging Pétain's input. In return, de Gaulle cavalierly paid the fulminating marshal no further heed. But even this revenge of 1938 for Pétain's intention of 1928 to steal his literary thunder—his sole, and precious, claim to fame at that juncture after a childhood spent fancying himself a great man and a young manhood spent training to be one—did not placate him down in the deep dark depths where grudges fester. For in 1958 he reversed what he had experienced in 1928 as Pétain's intended theft of his very person ("A book is a man," he had lamented then[27]). That is,

---

[24]Such ambivalence suggests Oedipal input. "Women, de Gaulle? The same ones as Pétain," François Mauriac knowingly affirmed of Lieutenant de Gaulle: Lacouture (1984): 50.
[25]Lacouture (1984): 145.
[26]Lacouture (1984): 276.
[27]Lacouture (1984): 144.

de Gaulle in 1958 literally took a leaf from Pétain's historic book when he demanded the same constituent powers as Pétain in 1940 in the same terms as Pétain in 1940 while refusing to acknowledge Pétain as his source. Unconsciously he did unto Pétain tit-for-tat what, thirty years before, he had blown up at Pétain for intending to do unto him: to attach his own name to the other's historic handiwork.

High as was de Gaulle's stake in May–June 1958 in the traumatic reliving of the French regime change of July 1940, that stake was personal before being national. Besides, even his adroit control over the process was limited. Not only did the regime change of 1958 replicate the key elements of its 1940 prototype, but it came with the telltale feel of fatality that was its traumatic birthmark. As early as 16 May 1958 Pétain's defence lawyer from his post-war trial told the Chambre: "Ladies and gentlemen, these may be the last days of the Fourth Republic."[28] A student agitator against de Gaulle's return later recollected: "Force was useless; surrender was a foregone conclusion."[29] One by one, without consulting their constituencies, the key party and parliamentary leaders, the premier, and the president of the Republic came around to de Gaulle as if by some dynamic inherent in the crisis.

Those who relived in concert in 1958 were, then, I repeat, the government and the parliament, with the country as a whole outside the loop just as it had been in 1940. They it was—the government and the parliament—who brought the regime into disfavour again toward 1958 as in the late 1930s and who let the pressures on it build up until de Gaulle was the sole recourse. And—here is the crucial point, hard to see clearly on first, second, and even third glance—that relived trauma was not the military debacle of May-June 1940, but the regime suicide that ensued. Or better, the relived trauma was the regime suicide as a derivative of the military debacle. Those who committed that regime suicide in July 1940 later claimed that they had been tricked[30]—a vintage childish form of denial. Indeed, trauma works childishly. Imagine some children whose house has collapsed over their heads and who, panicked, run for protection and comfort to a strong and kindly looking old soldier who turns

[28]Jacques Isorni, in *Débats*, 2366.

[29]Winock (1978): 209.

[30]Noguères (1955): 139–169; Paxton (1972): 24–33.

out to be vain-glorious, inept, and treacherous; they say he tricked them, but they know better at bottom, for in due course they contrive to relive their own panicked surrender. Just that childishly the government and parliament of May–June 1958 contrived to relive the panicked surrender by the government and parliament of June–July 1940—with, though, of all things, a happy outcome this time round.

The return of de Gaulle was, then, a disguised return of Pétain, a traumatic replay of June–July 1940 by the political establishment of May–June 1958. This traumatic replay presents several psychohistorical novelties as far as my own and, I think, others' previous researches have gone. For one, the Bordeaux–Vichy governmental and parliamentary trauma of June–July 1940 was a spinoff of the national trauma of defeat, which, however, did not enter into the replay in its own right. What the politicos later re-enacted was not the fall of France, but their specific traumatic sideshow, the fall of the Third Republic, just as through the fall of the Fourth Republic de Gaulle too later re-staged in reverse his own specific sideshow, Pétain's intended theft of his identity in 1928. As for the nationwide shock of the German onslaught in 1940, it was nowhere discernible in 1958—not even in the negative on a small scale through the country's failure to panic at the armed threat from Algiers.

Another, equally intriguing novelty of the replay with de Gaulle in 1958 cast as Pétain in 1940 is that the corporate body that did the replaying, the parliament with its dependent government, had undergone a nearly complete turnover in membership in the eighteen-year interim. This singularity throws into sharp relief the theoretical question of how a group trauma gets transmitted down the years or, in some cases, down the decades or centuries. Earlier studies of traumatic reliving *en groupe* have all dealt with whole nations or whole continents composed by and large of the same people, or their descendants, from trauma to reliving to eventual re-reliving, so that some form of transmission of the traumatic impact could be tacitly supposed. I stress "tacitly" as, for my part, I have always expressly distinguished the known fact of transmission from the unknown means of transmission, my preferred analogy being with the fact of gravitation, undisputed since Newton, as against its mode of transmission, first tentatively (and inconclusively) defined by quantum field theory over three centuries later. Nonetheless, for all my dismissal on principle over the years of the issue of transmission, I did secretly suspect some epigenetic mechanism or other at work. Now that misconceived suspicion is refuted.

I have saved for the last the most entertaining psychohistorical oddity about this incident of group traumatic reliving. In no other such case could I discover any individual awareness within the group of the reliving underway, however obsessively the trauma being relived may itself have been recalled in the process. On this score, let me quote some earlier words of my own that I shall promptly eat. In a lecture of 1990 I presented Romanticism as a European reliving of the Europe-wide trauma of the revolutionary dream of 1789 turning into the revolutionary nightmare of 1793–1794, whereupon in the course of my conclusion I remarked that "it was not contradictory for the Romantics to relive the failed Revolution unconsciously with that Revolution in mind: in traumatic reliving it is the fact of reliving, and not the thing being relived, that is unconscious".[31] So in researching how the Fourth Republic fell to de Gaulle in 1958 as the Third Republic had fallen to Pétain in 1940 I was hardly surprised to find continual allusions to 1940 in the 1958 run-up to de Gaulle's investiture. At a secret meeting called by President René Coty with de Gaulle and the leaders of the two houses of parliament on 28 May 1958 André Le Troquer of the Chambre drove de Gaulle to tears by citing the Vichy precedent behind de Gaulle's terms for returning. In the parliamentary debates meanwhile, deputies kept noting the incongruity that Pétain's first great adversary of 1940 was being backed by so many former Pétainists in 1958. It struck the Socialist leader Guy Mollet that de Gaulle evidently imagined in 1958 that he was back in 1940 again, opposing an illegitimate government.[32] Communist hecklers were quick to call the 1958 de Gaulle a fascist like the 1940 Pétain. But in such allusions Vichy was ever a polemical referent, never an acknowledged presence—never, that is, until an eleventh-hour intervention in the constitutional debate by the rightist lawyer and deputy Jean-Louis Tixier-Vignancourt. Tixier had voted for Pétain at Vichy, and then served the Pétain regime. He was to run against de Gaulle for president in 1965, scoring 5.27% of the first ballot, only to throw his support behind his friend and

[31] Binion (1990): 129.
[32] République Française, Assemblée Nationale, 16 May (1958): 2368.

erstwhile political confederate François Mitterrand in the runoff. On the issue of de Gaulle's Pétain-like bid for constituent powers on 2 June 1958 Tixier spoke directly to the new head of government, who, sitting wrapped in proud silence, vouchsafed him only a single "sign of denegation".[33] I shall quote Tixier's intervention at great length (although omitting most of the numerous interjections) because it shattered my prior understanding of group traumatic reliving as unconscious to all concerned.[34] Not only was Tixier aware of the reliving underway, but he was even privy to the permutation principle involved, as will be seen.

"*Monsieur le président du conseil,*" Tixier began,

> this evening's session reminds me of another one. I have before my eyes the draft by which you ask our Assembly to delegate its constituent power to the government you head on the understanding that the constitution to be drawn up by that government will be ratified by the nation through a referendum. In addition, an advisory committee chosen from parliament will be consulted. Such is the text before us.
>
> Monsieur le président du conseil, yesterday I voted for your investiture. This morning I voted for the full powers you sought. But this evening ... it will be impossible for me to vote to delegate the fraction of constituent power conferred on me by universal suffrage. Here is why. Some years ago you assembled a commission of jurists, among them, if memory serves, Monsieur Edgar Faure, whom I am pleased to see here at his bench. ... Now, this committee advised all of us deputies and senators of the Third Republic who on 10 July 1940 had voted for a motion stipulating that the Government would draw up a constitution to be ratified by the nation and applied by the chambres it would create, that we had no right to delegate this constituent power and that we had therefore—580 deputies and senators—committed a grave fault that warranted our being penalized with ineligibility. ... I understand, monsieur le président du conseil, that in the

[33] République Française, Assemblée Nationale, 2 June (1958): 2618.
[34] Yet again, I wonder at my prior *mis*understanding that Tixier's intervention shattered, for in my "Bush's America Goes To War", *Clio's Psyche*, X (2003), 1–3, I myself claimed to see my own country reliving its Twin Towers trauma through Shock and Awe.

present grave circumstances you should have felt the need to launch this appeal to the Chambre and tomorrow the Senate. I can see that. But you will excuse me if I would never have believed that twice in my existence I would be asked to delegate the fraction of constituent power that I held and, to top it off, if I never could have imagined that the second time I would be asked to do so by the very person who punished me for having granted this delegation a first time.

Edgar Faure: Monsieur Tixier-Vignancourt, may I interrupt you?

Jean-Louis Tixier-Vignancourt: Gladly.

Edgar Faure: ... I own that the question of delegating constituent power is a delicate one. But, Monsieur Tixier-Vignancourt, as in searching our memories we doubtless followed the same path at least up to a point, it happens that I have with me this evening a review published in Algiers at the time, when I had the honor, monsieur le président du conseil, of directing the legislative services of the committee of national liberation.

Jean-Louis Tixier-Vignancourt: I knew you had brought this review.

Edgar Faure: According to this text, our main criticism of the delegation of constituent power in Vichy was that it provided for the constitution to be ratified by the assemblies that it would itself create and that would apply it.

Jean-Louis Tixier-Vignancourt: Wrong!

Edgar Faure: So I must say ... that was something quite different from the referendum being proposed now. Since you alluded to my opinion, allow me to quote from this text: 'As for the provision for ratification by assemblies, it can only be seen as a mockery in that these assemblies are to be chosen arbitrarily at some unspecified date.' I felt the need to point out this essential difference. The constituent power belongs to the Assembly only by delegation from the people; hence [our] referendum provision, to consider that alone, returns the constituent power to its source.

Jean-Louis Tixier-Vignancourt: Very interesting. First I thank Monsieur Edgar Faure for his intervention. Then I congratulate our colleagues who confidently applauded him, for in the commentary he did in Algiers on the text adopted on 10 July 1940 Monsieur Edgar Faure made a fundamental mistake. He based his juridical exercise on the Government's draft, which was later revised at the prompting of a group of veterans from the Senate and some deputies ... . They raised exactly the same objection to that text. For the constitution to be ratified by assemblies that it created was a mockery, they said. That is why ratification by the nation—that is, by referendum—was introduced before the National Assembly met. That is also why, Monsieur le président Edgar Faure, your commentary in Algiers was worthless, as it was based only on a draft and not on the text that had been adopted.

Paul Ramadier: May I interrupt you?

Jean-Louis Tixier-Vignancourt: Please do, especially as we too have some memories in common.

Paul Ramadier: Monsieur Tixier-Vignancourt, it remains that the constitutional texts were to be applied before any ratification ...

Jean-Louis Tixier-Vignancourt: No!

Paul Ramadier: ... without having been submitted in any which way to any instance derived from universal suffrage.

Jean-Louis Tixier-Vignancourt: Wrong!

Paul Ramadier: That is where violence was done to national sovereignty, to the sovereignty of universal suffrage.

Jean-Louis Tixier-Vignancourt: No! I thank Monsieur Ramadier for his intervention anyhow.

President [of the Assembly]: Let's not reconvene the commission of jurists that sat in Algiers!

Jean-Louis Tixier-Vignancourt: Monsieur le président, you will allow us, I am sure, in a debate sufficiently important to each of us because of the vote to be cast, to examine in full the only existing precedent of the sort in the annals of the deliberative assemblies of the Republic. President Ramadier, I beg leave to remind you that the text adopted expressly provided for no application of the constitution before its ratification by the nation, since it was worded as follows: 'It will be ratified by the nation and applied by the assemblies it will have created.' ... And that is why, my dear colleagues, as I told you at the outset, I cannot, in the same conditions as eighteen years ago—I'm sorry, but this debate has proven that the conditions are exactly the same ...

Maurice Schumann: The same?

Jean-Louis Tixier-Vignancourt: Yes, Monsieur Maurice Schumann,

> the conditions are the same, except perhaps, to your mind, that the vote of 10 July 1940 followed a military defeat. This evening's vote follows—otherwise it wouldn't be taking place, you surely agree—multiple, successive political defeats that wind up being equivalent, alas! to the greatest of all setbacks.

After a final refusal to replay along, Tixier took a parting shot at his audience: "Protest all you like! It's true and you know it."[35]

None of Tixier-Vignancourt's indignant contradictors, let alone their loud supporters, remembered the incriminated Vichy text straight even after it was recalled to them straight: they were in total denial.[36] The 1958 text, as Tixier rightly contended, was congruent with its 1940 original, which de Gaulle had opposed for all he was worth. The re-enactment in progress was accordingly a political about-face, or reversal, on de Gaulle's part. And Tixier topped off his *explication de vote* in terms of what I have called (adapting Lévi-Strauss's usage) "permutation"—the principle of surface substitutes for key elements of a trauma being relived. As Tixier had it, the circumstances in 1958 were, *mutatis mutandis*, the same as in 1940, with "multiple, successive political defeats" as of 1958 standing in for the military defeat of 1940. By those "multiple, successive political defeats" Tixier presumably meant the loss of Indochina, Morocco, and Tunisia, possibly the Suez War too, and prospectively Algeria. In none of these cases, not even in Indochina, had French arms failed as previously in 1940, but, as seen from Tixier's right-wing vantage point, French politics and diplomacy were losing what French arms were not. I would sooner stress other equivalences between 1940 and 1958, beginning with immediate outside pressure on the Assembly in both cases—the pressure that Mendès France so eloquently denounced in his own *explication de vote* against de Gaulle. But then, Tixier had a right-wing agenda far removed from my scholarly concern.

---

[35] République Française, Assemblée Nationale, 16 May (1958): 2618–20.

[36] Assemblée Nationale (1947): 502; further, ibid., 69–70 (Marin), 112 (Herriot). Even René Rémond in *Le retour de de Gaulle*, while recognizing that the Vichy precedent obsessed the deputies debating the constituent powers for de Gaulle (20, 104, 168–69), gets that precedent wrong (10 4–105). Rousso (1987): 81–83, credits Tixier-Vignancourt with clever polemics if nothing else. Jäckel (1958): 490–504, esp. 498–503, came closest to recognizing the 1940 = 1958 parallel.

René Rémond concludes his fine political monograph *Le retour de de Gaulle* by stressing the contingent nature of de Gaulle's sudden triumphal reemergence from political obsolescence—the concurrence of several flukes, chief among them President René Coty's unexampled threat to resign unless his appointment of de Gaulle was confirmed.[37] By contrast, psychohistorical analysis tends to suggest a forced run of events along a pre-set trajectory: the Third French Republic having self-destructed traumatically in 1940 at the height of a national catastrophe, its later close copy, the Fourth French Republic, looks, with psychohistorical hindsight, fated to self-destruct in turn under equivalent conditions of its own devising. That it did just that is, I think, amply evident. That it had to do just that is, however, a retrospective optical illusion, despite the strain of compulsion involved in the mechanism of reliving. For one thing, a trauma need not be relived. Whether a given trauma ever gets relived instead of being obsessively remembered, or defended against after the fact,[38] or worked up into a fixed symptom, or just obstinately denied, depends on a large number of unpredictables such as, in the present case, the availability of a national hero of a stature comparable to Pétain's. For another, a reliving has a pick of acceptable equivalents to any element of its traumatic original: thus many another outside threat to the Fourth Republic could have served as well as the one from the self-proclaimed committee of public safety in Algiers. And again, the felicitous outcome of de Gaulle's investiture on his Pétainist terms—above all, a new republican constitution that fast laid all his opponents' fears to rest—was by no means a foregone conclusion; quite the contrary.

For all that, political history, or indeed history of whatever kind, is less contingent than it appears in non-psychohistorical perspective. In our example again, once the mechanism of reliving kicked in, Pierre Pflimlin was bound to resign as head of government in 1958 the way Paul Reynaud had resigned in 1940, without being voted out, and President René Coty was bound to appoint de Gaulle next

[37] Rémond (1987): 164–168.

[38] The Fourth Republic also defended after the fact against the fall of the Third in the long run-up to reliving it: hyper-fearful of personal empowerment, it constitutionally maximized the control of the chambers over the government and asserted that control continually thereafter by toppling ministries in quick succession.

in 1958 the way President Albert Lebrun had appointed Pétain next in 1940, overriding the leaders of the two chambres. As for de Gaulle-1958 cast as Pétain-1940, how could he resist swiping a leaf from the historic Pétain, who had traumatically sought to steal his identity in 1925–1928 through that ghostwritten book about the French soldier in history ("A book is a man")? The bottom line is that even under outside pressure people act, or react, as they are inwardly impelled to act or react. Such inward impulsion, whether of individuals or groups, may be flexible as to its mode of discharge or in its choice of outlets. But it, and it alone, is the active principle of history. There is no explaining de Gaulle's return or his recall to power in 1958 without considering what inwardly impelled him to return and, likewise, what inwardly impelled the political establishment to recall him. The closer one examines both inner pressures in their interplay, the less accident-prone history proves to be.

At their height, such inner pressures can convey a sense of necessitation akin to the ancient notion of fate. This notion, refuted over and again, simply won't go away. Its sticking power against all reason argues a tenacious subjective reality behind it. And what tenacious subjective reality fills the bill better than a trauma-driven inner imperative that overrides convenience, judgement, and conscience alike? At any rate, the inner imperative of traumatic reliving is a prime source of the notion of fate in imaginative literature, where it has been most powerfully rendered. To traumatic reliving in fiction I therefore turn next.

CHAPTER FIVE

Reliving in letters

Let us back up before broaching traumatic reliving in *belles lettres*.[1]

Freud put mental trauma on the clinical agenda in the 1890s, when he took neurosis to be a mix of old "traumas", meaning loosely emotional tensions, stresses, or upsets, relived in disguise. Toward 1900 his focus gradually shifted away from relatively recent "traumas", or pathogenic material such as he had been finding behind neuroses, to their presumed infantile originals. Psychoanalytical trauma theory followed this same turn to infantile originals even though the earmark of a trauma proper is that it has no original. The psychiatric diagnostic category "post-traumatic stress disorder", introduced in the 1980s, has confused the subject further by taking bodily violence suffered, threatened, or witnessed, followed by incessant, anxious recall or else by defensive memory blackout, to be the standard traumatic syndrome. Here psychiatry is wrong. As historic case studies of individual traumatic reliving show, a purely emotional upset can traumatize on a par with an experience of bodily violence. The effect of either is of a blow too hard to be taken in

[1]This chapter has been adapted from Binion (2008): 10–18, and Binion (2008b): 11–20.

stride that inflicts a wound too deep to heal on its own. The blow may indeed be incessantly remembered, in pain and dread, either waking or sleeping, particularly in response to outside reminders. But it may instead be memorialized with the affect controlled or repressed. Or else the affect may recur in eerie isolation, detached from any recollection of its source; thus a clinical study of episodic hypertension attributes it "in almost every single case" to traumatic anxiety relived unconsciously.[2] Again, the blow may be defended against after the fact beyond all useful purpose without the original experience in mind. It may equally well enter into a chronic symptom, like a steady headache from a scary bang on the head. Finally, it may appear to be more or less absorbed except that, long months or years afterwards, the sufferer contrives to relive it unawares together with the key elements of the attendant experience. In this last case, the original experience itself may well be remembered in the process, but then with no connection drawn to the reliving underway. The most recognition a reliving normally gets in its own time or afterwards is just an unfocused déjà vu. As Ernest Hemingway put it for a traumatized narrator, "I had the feeling as in a nightmare of its all being something repeated, something I had been through and that now I must go through again."[3] This creepy feeling is about as close to consciousness as an individual reliving ever comes.

Take this option of unsuspecting, contrived reliving, add a dash of fantasy, and vast poetic-dramatic prospects open up. Those prospects have actually been pursued since antiquity. Fiction notoriously privileges intense, often horrific, experiences. The reliving of such experiences in fiction ought to be notorious too by the same token, for it can be as riveting as traumatic reliving is in real life.

I propose to examine six literary classics built around individual traumatic reliving—one ancient, one medieval, one baroque, two romantic, and a modern one dating from shortly before psychoanalysis hit the world of letters. Once Freud caught on with fictionists, unconscious purposes in fiction lost their theoretical innocence. Freud's schema, as we have seen, precluded traumatic reliving. Nonetheless, Freudian influence cannot be ruled out for even such original twentieth-century masterworks of traumatic

---

[2]Mann (1998): 97.
[3]Hemingway (1926): 71.

reliving as Luigi Pirandello's *Six Characters in Search of an Author* and *Henry IV*, Ernest Hemingway's *The Sun Also Rises*, William Butler Yeats's *Purgatory*, Tennessee Williams's *Orpheus Descending*, Friedrich Dürrenmatt's *The Visit*, Harold Pinter's *Old Times*, or most recently Israel Horovitz's *The Widow's Blind Date*, free though each one is of childhood referents for the traumas that they show being relived. In any case, my six pre-Freudian specimens turn on relived traumas posited naively, not as applied theory. None of the six argues, let alone conceptualizes, traumatic reliving, although it informs all six equally. In each and all of them it is a dramatic device first and last. For this very reason it could not have scored as it did without striking a resonant note in a receptive public. It is this resonant note that I hope to sound out of the six works taken together. But first I must present them one by one.

To present the first of these six works I need to digress at the very outset. A few years ago I argued that traumatic reliving was the inside story of Sophocles' *Oedipus the King* and, I added, of it alone in classic Greek letters as far as the records disclose.[4] My argument about Sophocles' masterwork itself stands. Its hero twice relives a primal trauma reconfigured. "This trauma"—to quote my introductory summation—"is the one that he suffered when, because of a prophecy, he was thrust from his home in Thebes into exile before he was a full three days old. Some twenty years later he fled his adoptive home in Corinth into exile in Thebes because of that same prophecy somewhat elaborated. This was a classic reliving, with only the geographic reversal to disguise it. On stage, Oedipus relives the same trauma another twenty-odd years later when he goes into exile yet again from his home in Thebes because of that very same prophecy, now fulfilled."[5] Although I have had no second thoughts about the ensuing argument in all its complex detail, no sooner did I see it in print than I rued my incautious addendum to it about the singularity in the classic Greek corpus of this use of traumatic reliving by Sophocles. I had lost sight of Euripides' *Ion* of c. 410 BC, the one other extant Greek foundling play.[6] It too turns on the reliving long years afterwards of a neonate's traumatic exposure, only in *Ion*

[4]Binion (1997): 18.
[5]Binion (1997): 10.
[6]Giannopoulou (2000): 269.

the reliver is the exposer rather than the exposed. In both works a mother has had to abandon her firstborn, a son, who nevertheless survives to find his way back to her some twenty years later, Apollo having connived at his fate all the while. In both works, furthermore, the mother has been barren since exposing the boy, and in both she promptly recovers her fertility when he returns. Amusingly, as if to round out the parallels (geometry be damned), *Ion* followed *Oedipus the King* by about twenty years, which was roughly the length of the interval between trauma and reliving in both plays as also, for good measure, between the first and second reliving by Sophocles' Oedipus. As for divergences between the two works, the sharpest one is that Sophocles scaled tragic heights in *Oedipus the King* whereas Euripides dipped deep into farce in whole chunks of *Ion*.

Naturalism vies with supernaturalism throughout Euripides' fabulous *tour de force*. In the back story Creusa, princess and later queen of Athens, was brutally raped by Apollo in her youth. A son resulted whom she bore in secret and tearfully exposed. She then married Xuthus, a valiant warrior allied to Athens. The on-stage action begins long years afterwards as the seasoned royal couple, childless despite their "longing for children"[7], visit the shrine of Apollo to ask why. Guarding the shrine is Creusa's son, its Delphic priestess having found and raised him by Apollo's devising. Now Apollo undertakes to manoeuvre the lad into his mother's home and arms without betraying her traumatic secret. Thus Apollo's oracle persuades gullible Xuthus that he fathered the foundling at a Dionysian fling in his bachelorhood. Delighted, Xuthus names him Ion and plans to take him home to Athens as a simple guest before gently breaking the supposed truth to Creusa. But the visit to Apollo's shrine has put Creusa for her part in such pained memory of her rape and its lacerating sequel that it takes only an old family slave twisting hints from the Chorus to convince her that Xuthus sired his alleged guest adulterously with a slave girl and reared him in secret so as to steal the throne of Athens for his own breed. Enraged, Creusa again strikes out at the unwelcome bastard, this time with a vengeance as is the traumatic way. Again her intent miscarries, and Ion mobilizes Athens to stone or hurl her to death. She seeks refuge at Apollo's altar, where in the nick of time she

[7]Euripides (c. 410 B.C.).

recognizes the foundling's old wrappings brought by the nurturant priestess. A joyous mother–son reunion ensues, and Creusa, detraumatized, promptly recovers her fertility within a marriage thenceforth subject to a multiplex deception on her part: besides still keeping her godly rape and ensuing maternity secret from Xuthus, she must now indulge Xuthus in his fond false belief, at once joyous and apologetic, that he is Ion's father. This messy happy ending announced by Athena as *dea ex machina* is the more farcical in that Creusa is de-sterilized by dint of learning that she no longer needs an heir.

That Creusa's godly rape was meant as traumatic weeps out of Euripides' verses. Creusa recalls it with pathetic immediacy when she reminds Apollo through the female Chorus: "Grabbing hold of my white wrists, you led me to a bed on a cave floor while I shrieked 'Mother!'" But it is her exposure of her resultant child out of shame and fear that was the supreme traumatic moment for her, again as fully present and painful all those long years afterwards as on the fateful day itself. At Apollo's temple she slowly unties her inner wraps on the festering sore spot so far as to tell Ion mournfully about a fictive girlfriend who abandoned her firstborn: "Poor little child! ... She went back to where she left him—and he was gone." Apostrophizing Apollo afterwards, she recalls outright how "in dread of my mother's eye, with many tears I laid him on the same cruel bed where you ravished me". And she asks: "Where is he now, our little child?" Then for the first time she tells her old slave of her bruising brush with divinity and its sorrowful issue, concluding: "I left him there in the cave—how could I bear to do it? I said my pitiful good-bye to him, steeling my heart to cruelty." When the loving old confidant ventures: "Cruel! But Apollo was crueler," she concurs only to castigate herself as well, as if still in shock at abandoning her son: "You would have said so if you had seen him stretch out his hands to me, reaching for my breast, feeling for my arms, wanting his rightful place, which I took from him." When later, upon their climactic happy reunion, Ion asks her: "Mother, how could you do it?" she replies: "I was in the grip of terror."

Such spaced quotations as these from *Ion* actually understate my point. Throughout the play the focus is unfailingly on Creusa traumatized, then de-traumatized. Its "central motif", to quote a textual exegete of Euripides, is the exposure of Ion as Creusa both recalls and relives it.[8] Four times the wrenching event that she had hitherto kept to herself in solitary remorse is recounted.[9] As her memory of it revives in full force, so do the anxiety and shame that prompted her reluctant deed. To take the anxiety first, it looms gigantic in—to quote the same authority further—

> the psychological substratum ... [of her later] attempt on her unrecognized son's life (cf. l. 1300: ... μ' ἀπέκτειυες φόβω). Thus Euripides suggests a parallel between the motivation of Creusa's abandonment of her child so many years ago and the psychological motives of the present abortive murder. A similar association between the remote past and the present is made for the other motive of the ἔκθεσις [exposure], shame. ... Shame has not only led her to conceal her pregnancy and childbirth, even from her loyal servant, and to remove her new-born child, but it has deterred her for many years from telling this traumatic experience to anybody. Only in the course of the play itself do the barriers of this shame break down. In her first conversation with Ion, αιδώς [shame] still restrains her: therefore she twice interrupts her account and hides her own affair behind the fictitious adventure of a friend. But she entreats Ion to conceal even this invented story from her husband. Only when her tormented soul suffers a new blow, viz. the oracle giving Xuthus a full-grown son but seemingly leaving her without offspring, does she finally abandon all inhibitions.[10]

More, just like the themes of anxiety and shame at the time of the exposure and again within the action of the play, so too is the theme of secrecy

> explicitly exploited by Euripides to draw a connection between the crucial event of child abandonment and the present attempt on [Ion's] life. This shows how skillfully the tragedian has integrated the traditional motives for the ἔκθεσις [exposure], fear

---

[8]Huys (1995): 13.
[9]Huys (1995): 94.
[10]Huys (1995): 97–98. (For consistency's sake I am changing Huys's spelling from Kreousa and Xouthos.)

> and shame, with the correlative secrecy, into the action of the play. Creusa's emotions are essential not only for the motivation of her deed many years ago, but also of her present murderous attempt. ... The journey to Delphi where her memories of Apollo again become vivid, and the terrible oracle depriving her definitively, as she falsely believes, of a child, kindle her old grief so long suppressed by αιδώς [shame]. This psychological shock, reflecting her panic at the moment of the ἔκθεσις [exposure], culminates in the rash attack against Ion by which she unknowingly endangers the life of her son for the second time.[11]

Her trauma thereby leads "to a violent escalation"[12] as she relives it. It remains only to specify that, while she relives it wholly in its grip, she does not for all that even suspect the reliving underway.

Superficially seen, Creusa cannot be reliving her traumatic exposure of baby Ion when she tries to kill grown-up Ion, as she identifies grown-up Ion with baby Ion only afterwards. Unsuperficially seen, however, this is just where Euripides' genius shines brightest: in establishing the emotional equivalence of Creusa's initial relationship to grown-up Ion with her earlier agonized tenderness toward her secret, lost baby. The feel of Apollo's temple prompts her tormented return in spirit to the ground of her trauma. She weeps upon first encountering grown-up Ion there, for, she explains, the site has stirred up "an old memory" in her. Ion shortly chances to mention—on cue, as it were—Apollo's rocks where she was raped and where she later exposed their child. Her old pain revives anew because, as she puts it, "the caves there hold a certain shameful secret that I know of". Her barren marriage comes up, and Ion asks: "You never bore any child all your life?" She evades that one affectionately: "Your mother is to be envied." Ion counters that he was a foundling "never nursed at the breast". "Poor child!" she exclaims, "you have suffered as I have"—and (subtlest touch of all) Ion lets this allusion to her trauma over and beyond her later childlessness pass as if he understood it. The two enter into still closer tacit intelligence

---

[11] Huys (1995): 99.
[12] Huys (1995): 148.

as Creusa cries: "Your poor mother! I wonder who she was," and Ion ventures: "Some woman who was wronged, perhaps." With mother and son both now back in their thoughts at the mutually traumatic moment, she exposes herself to him transparently: "Someone who has suffered the same fate as your mother," she tells him, fell prey to Apollo, abandoned the resultant baby boy, returned to search the spot, found no trace of him, and is now dying to learn his fate. "How long has it been?" asks Ion. Right on target Creusa replies: "If he were alive he would be just your age." Ion embraces her inwardly: "How sad! What you tell me echoes my own sadness." Creusa reciprocates: "You too—yes! Some poor mother must be longing for you." Euripides even pushes the inner rapport between them so far as to have Ion once call that fictive woman's case "your case" (Creusa rectifies only hesitantly: "her case"). With surpassing artistry, then, Euripides casts grown-up Ion straight off as in Creusa's heart the beloved child she wanted to kill. To cite a second expert opinion on this encounter: "Between Ion and Creusa there is a natural sympathy, a kind of unconscious recognition of their real but unknown relationship."[13] By the time that brief scene is over, Ion's exposure in infancy as Creusa hears of it has fused with her trauma of exposing him in infancy as she remembers it. This "sensitive and tactful"[14] maternal–filial bond is thrown into still sharper relief by Ion's chilly, mocking reaction when Xuthus intrudes on the scene claiming to be his father, and then climactically by her own subsequent trauma-driven, blood-thirsty attempt on Ion's life.

What triggers this attempt is the prank Apollo plays with Xuthus. Too crafty by half, it could not fail to sting Creusa to the quick so long as she was not privy to it. When Xuthus calls Ion his son, Ion sensibly says of Creusa: "She will hate me, and rightly. When she has no son, how could she endure to see me stand next to my father's throne?" Indeed, when she hears the news she wants to "soar up through the melting sky, far from the land of Greece beyond the Western stars". The compassionate female Chorus laments: "There will be tears for this ... when the Queen sees him happy with his son, and knows herself left childless and alone." And the Chorus pursues, apostrophizing Apollo: "Why wrap up your chanted word

---

[13]Cronacher (1967): 268.
[14]Cronacher (1967): 282.

in mystery? Who is this youth reared in your temple halls? In whose womb did he lie? I do not like your answer: it rings false. ... There's trickery here!" For all its impious suspicion of Apollo, the Chorus turns against Xuthus ("Curse him, traitor, curse him!") and by ricochet against Ion ("Let his new life be death to him!"). To Creusa the Chorus construes the oracle as that she will never have children, and she cries: "Oh! Let me die!" and again: "This answer has broken my heart, I cannot bear it, I will not live!" And when next, adding divine insult to divine injury, the Chorus tells her that Apollo has given Xuthus a son, she moans: "Oh! This is the bitterest of all!" Then it is that the old slave, augmenting Apollo's malevolence, slanders Xuthus: "He went behind your back to some slave-woman, and from her got this boy." The Chorus chimes in with this slander even though it has witnessed how guileless Xuthus exulted at finding himself a father by some forgotten bacchante of his bachelor days. Gripped by pity for Creusa, it even backs the old slave in urging her to murder Xuthus and Ion both.

Why does Euripides' Apollo let Creusa be so bitterly misled by his oracle about Ion's parentage? For that matter, why has he let her eat her heart out in solitary remorse over her lost son through so many long years of barren marriage? The answer is at once short and weighty: to set her up for reliving—for a reprise of her first, traumatic attempt on Ion's life. Note what feeble evidence of Xuthus's treachery suffices to arouse her fierce vengefulness misdirected against Ion. When the outraged old slave bids her "Take your revenge!" after she recounts her traumatic rape and child exposure, she brushes aside both Apollo and Xuthus as prospective targets to snatch at innocent Ion instead—a politic choice except that she is not choosing politically. The slave first suggests burning Apollo's temple, and she begs off. Next he urges: "Kill your husband," and she objects incongruously that "he has been a good husband to me in the past"—she who has only just exclaimed: "My husband has turned traitor!" That leaves only Ion, and she shrieks for his death with unseemly promptitude and ferocity. Thus it takes no more than a slave's nasty hunch about Xuthus for her to move against Ion's life a second time. That she strikes out so rashly at Ion, and the Chorus with her, just goes to show how unproblematic, how much a mere fact of life, traumatic reliving was for Euripides and presumably also for his public. Creusa was not acting out a psychological mechanism; rather, I am spelling out a psychological mechanism that the playwright evidently just took for granted.

Creusa promptly recovers her fertility when she finds her exposed son alive and learns of Apollo's invisible hand in his very exposure—when her fear and guilt dissolve. Hence her sterility had been due to her traumatic abandonment of her infant son rather than to any impact of her rape. Or did Euripides intend a curative effect of her reliving? Hardly. Athena tells Creusa at the end, after enumerating Ion's children to come: "You and Xuthus too shall have sons." If this seeming afterthought was Apollo's will, as would follow from its utterance in his temple, what did the trick was not the reliving, which Apollo did not intend, but the reunion, which he did. To the same effect, Creusa's opposite number, Sophocles' Jocasta, did not relive but did likewise recover her fertility after her reunion with her own exposed son.

Much is messy in *Ion*, beginning with Apollo's farcical scheme itself. According to Hermes in the prologue, the point of this scheme was "that the boy may come to his mother's house, and be recognized by her, and receive the position due to his birth, without any exposure of her union with Apollo"—that is, of her maternity of Ion. According to Athena in the epilogue, on the other hand, Apollo had intended to reveal Ion as Creusa's son after a mere brief spell as Xuthus's. But then by going public in Athens with Creusa's maternity of Ion, Apollo would have shown that he had played Xuthus for a fool besides raising the touchy question of Ion's paternity. Wiser Athena admonishes Creusa: "Now, tell no one Ion is your true son, so that Xuthus may enjoy his delusion, and you may enjoy the happiness you know to be yours." She gives Ion no hint, however, of what to tell the Delphic populace howling for Creusa's death. As for how Creusa can conceal her intense relationship with Ion indefinitely even from obtuse Xuthus, or for that matter how for starters she could ever have passed herself off even to credulous Xuthus as a virgin after a rape and a childbirth—no way, but no matter. Those loose ends all take scrutiny of the script to spot. They will pass unnoticed in any apt staging of such an earthy, unearthly trauma being relived so breathtakingly close to the brink.

On from the earthy-unearthly to the ghostly subterranean. In his great poetic record of his imaginary visit to the afterworld, *The Divine Comedy* of about 1314, Dante relates that in the teeming pit of lust on the inner edge of hell he summoned the shades of Francesca da Rimini and her lover, Paolo, to recount their plight to him. Slain together by Francesca's husband, who caught them indulging their reciprocal passion, the two are being perpetually tossed about together, like other sinners of their ilk, by fierce winds forever rising and falling. In Dante's symbolic vision, their infernal situation represented their sin as its own punishment. The fierce winds were like lust at its height: no resistance availed against them as they blew their helpless victims up and down, round and round, in an arid parody of the sex act complete with breathers between successive rounds. For Dante, such forced reliving with a vengeance was not curative. As he saw it, souls could be purged of their sins not by symbolic overdosing but only by painful antidotes, as on the seventh terrace of purgatory, where lust is burned out of repentant brutish souls. It is hard to see how the lusty shades in hell can be wind-tossed, being immaterial: Francesca speaks of her fair body as having been "taken from me". Dante's imagery here is problematic also in that, in the theology of his day as of ours, submission is blameless where resistance is impossible, as to fierce winds of passion here or hereafter. Such winds, literalized in hell, are meant as punitive there in two ways at once. One way is tedious excess: although intermittent, they afford their victims no respite as compared with earthly lust, which yields to sleep if to nothing else. The other way is that their victims, being fleshless, cannot even feel, let alone enjoy, that nagging, engulfing sin of the flesh, now eternalized as a sin of the spirit. The torment is the greater for Francesca and her partner in that, having been traumatically slaughtered in sin together, they are traumatically stuck together forever while also bereft of the wherewithal to go on sinning. Had they loved instead of lusting, their eternal togetherness would be a deathless reward. However, in calling their lust by the fair name of love, they fool only the pilgrim Dante and not the poet Dante, let alone themselves or divine justice. So much was it lust that their adultery, albeit a more sinful sin, does not even figure in their guilt down under. Slain in the very act of lust, they must crave each other's missing flesh eternally out of eternal memory alone and in perpetual weariness of each other's spirit—hers devious, his vacuous.[15]

[15]See Binion (1997): 45–54.

Their torment is redoubled by what is peculiar to their case in that pit of lust as far as the poem indicates: that they were caught and slain in the act of lust, which left them eternally traumatized and eternally thwarted both at once. In the perspective of mortality, being slain precludes being traumatized. Not so in the poet's immortal perspective, with the afterlife abidingly focused on the life that it supposedly leaves behind but never does—the life that is in fact forever being relived, stripped down in each case to its crucial, defining feature. Just as they relive their lust perpetually in memory, so are these two hapless partners in sin eternally suspended in the fatal moment that cut their lust short. The poem singles them out to exemplify lust, and then defines them instead by their traumatic death. It is in blaming their "woeful fate" on that death rather than on themselves that Francesca identifies herself and Paolo in the first place to the Tuscan tourist in hell. In sum, the poem treats their afterlife as an eternal traumatic reliving, and at that as the eternal reliving of a trauma that is cut in two like the lovers themselves. That is, the frustrated carnal traffic is incessantly relived but not recalled—Francesca, who does all the talking, talks around and away from the lust that is the very reason for her dismal posthumous lot—while the murder is incessantly recalled but not relived. Or again, she both recalls and relives the trauma by halves: she recalls the murder and relives the frustrated lust. It may seem contradictory that the perpetual reliving for its part is imposed from the outside, by divine ordinance, rather than generated from within like the perpetual recall, but that is exactly how traumatic reliving is experienced: as a woeful outer fate.

What business has a traumatic reliving in this keynote canto of Dante's hell? Its business is Dante's own: to define and illustrate hell. For Dante, hell was earthbound in the pain and futility of eternal reliving. His damned souls all relive hereafter like traumatized worldlings, without aim and without end. This view of damnation would seem to have arisen out of the same human depths as traumatic reliving itself, which likewise has the unconscious feel of déjà vu and of no exit both at once. Like Dante's sinners, traumatic relivers are no penitents, but victims caught in a guilt trap that doubles as a recurrent punishment with the circularity of a loaded argument. And spent lust without love on earth—lust as a soulless repetitive craving with no aim or end beyond itself—is, like traumatic reliving, a foretaste of damnation in Dante's poetic justice, except that in damnation according to Dante the soulless craving is fleshless too for good measure.

Back to the pained fleshly realm with Racine's last play, *Athaliah* of 1690. Its editor in the authoritative Pléiade edition remarked that its genius was "foreign to the interior and psychological tragedy that [had] seemed to characterize Racine".[16] In point of fact *Athaliah* is more interior and psychological than any of Racine's other works. But it deals with a traumatic reliving that comes through as such only unconsciously to spectators or readers as also to its heroine. Consciously the traumatic reliving manifests in the surface guise of a premonition fulfilled. That premonition of Athaliah's takes the form of a nightmare.

Athaliah, widow of a king descended from David, rules Judah in the worship of Baal. Nine or ten years earlier, a henchman of the Jewish god slew first her son and then her mother, Jezebel, idolatrous queen of Israel, whose corpse he left to the dogs. Horrified, Athaliah reacted by ordering all her son's children massacred so as to exterminate the line of David. In Racine's conception, Athaliah was doubly, if also selectively, traumatized in the process: first by her mother's death, omitting her son's,[17] and then by her own wild and bloody reaction against the god of the Jews insofar as it struck her son's lastborn, infant son in particular. The two terms of her trauma are both already evoked by turns in the opening scene through an allusion to Jezebel's grim death with "the dogs' thirst slaked in her inhuman blood," then a chilling reminder that "Athaliah snuffed out the infant even in the cradle".[18] That infant, Joash, did not perish, however. Left for dead, he was secretly rescued by a stepdaughter of Athaliah's, whose husband, the Jewish high priest in Jerusalem, has raised him in the temple as an alleged foundling. Athaliah nervously suspects as much, as shows between the lines of her account of her nightmare to her high officer, Abner, and to the high priest of Baal. Because her account is the pivotal passage of this poetic drama of trauma relived, I shall render it at length in pentameters approximating Racine's suppler alexandrines:

---

[16] Racine (1690): 888.
[17] Racine herein departed from 2 Kings 11: "Now when Athaliah ... saw that her son was dead, she arose and destroyed all the royal family."
[18] Racine (1690): 898 (I:1).

Athaliah.
A dream—why should a dream upset me so?—
Keeps eating at my heart shot through with woe.
I flee it; it pursues me in my flight.
Deep was the horror of that endless night.
My mother, Jezebel, decked out in pride
And clad in pomp as on the day she died,
Appeared before me with no hint of ill.
She even wore her farded glitter still
Upon her face, that ornate painted charm
To hide the years' irreparable harm.
Tremble, she said, oh daughter of my heart,
You too the Jewish god will bring to nought.
I shudder at his fearful grip on you,
My daughter. Once her dire words were through
Her shadow seemed to bend down over me.
My hands reached out to meet it tenderly
Only to find a horrid mix of grime
With mangled flesh and bone dragged in the slime,
With bloody shreds, and ghastly limbs undone
That rabid dogs fought over in the sun.

Abner.

Dear God!

Athaliah.
Then to my eyes amid this mess
Came a young child cloaked in a stunning dress
Such as one sees the Hebrew preachers wear.
This sight revived my spirits from despair.
But as I quit my morbid mood and took
His sweetness in, his noble, modest look,
I felt quite suddenly that traitor thrust
A deadly metal deep into my breast.[19]

Athaliah relates further that the Joash sequence of this dream recurred a second night, whereupon she impulsively entered the Jewish temple and spotted her secreted dream child there before being evicted by the scandalized congregation.

---

[19] Racine (1690): 910–911 (II:v).

The offstage pre-play, recounted above, dominates the on-stage play once Athaliah tells her two counsellors about her ghastly dream. For that on-stage play is all about Athalia's contriving to relive both terms of her double trauma at once. She simultaneously replays her mother's death straight and her death order against Joash in reverse. This last she does by so provoking the Jews that their high priest has her slain on Joash's account. She affirms the replay in saying at the climax: "I recognize the spot where I had him struck," and by asking that "he be made to thrust the knife into my breast".[20] She even augments her intimacy with him from a grandmother's to a mother's when she adds redundantly: "This is what his mother wants from him in dying."[21] She had increased their intimacy this way once before when, shortly after relating her dream, she wondered aloud: "Where would I be today if, mastering my weakness,/ I had not muffled a mother's tenderness?"[22] As this muffled tenderness is what made her failed murder of Joash traumatic, it is pointed up again in her rich closing lines when she speaks of having acted "in spite of myself" (*"à moi-même opposée"*) against a child "arousing my remorse".[23] To the same effect of immediatizing the trauma, Racine had suggested earlier that Athaliah practically wielded the knife herself at the massacre of her grandchildren, and this notwithstanding the strict rules of classicist decorum forbidding lofty personages to sully their hands with any base or sordid business: "A dagger in her hand, implacable,/She goaded her rude soldiers to the carnage/And followed then its course."[24] To point up the reliving, Racine echoed the key phrase of this passage verbatim in the last act, where Athaliah is said to be approaching the temple "a dagger in her hand".[25] The traumatic measure was full.

That measure is spectrally rather than bloodily full in Edgar Allan Poe's *Ulalume* of 1847. This haunting ballad poetized a reliving in terms that conceal as much about it as they reveal while disclosing next to nothing about the horrendous trauma repeatedly intimated behind it. To take Poe's poetic narrator at his word, he found himself

---

[20] Racine (1690): 160 (V:vi).
[21] Racine (1690): (V:vi).
[22] Racine (1690): 920–921 (II:vii).
[23] Racine (1690): 959 (V:vi).
[24] Racine (1690): 902 (I:ii).
[25] Racine (1690): 951 (V:i).

roaming through a misty autumnal woodland one night, unaware that he had fatefully traversed that same autumnal woodland by night once before. Lava now flowed from his volcanic heart over deep-frozen memories. Drawn by a warm and lustrous crescent of stars, which promised him release from both guilt and remorse through love, he placated his mistrustful soul, personified as a foot-dragging Psyche, even as he advanced trance-like toward "the Lethean peace of the skies"—advanced facing skywards, that is, until he hit up with a jolt against a vault where his lost Ulalume lay buried. His single allusion to Ulalume's traumatic burial itself conveys the full equivalence, indeed the equation, for him of the replay with its traumatic original: "It was ... /On this very night of last year/ ... That I brought a dread burden down here." In brief, he outright conflated the two moments: in retrospect they were one and the same. In his mythopoeic scheme he surmises that some demon had been able to tempt him back to "the thing that lies hidden in these wolds" only because merciful ghouls had well-meaningly cloaked the lusty goddess Astarte's "sinfully scintillant" star in Diana's chaste moonlight for that sly purpose. More prosaically put, his demonic drive to relive, disguised as the lure of a restorative new love, had overridden his inner apprehensions.

This loony, lyrical monologue conveys the subjective experience of traumatic reliving with unique intensity and connotative power. It starkly renders the fluid form and trance-like feel of it—of rerunning a fateful, fatal traumatic course with deep foreboding the whole way. Equally in keeping with that form and that feel, it leaves largely blank the corresponding facts, beginning with the specifics of Ulalume's burial. Just as a traumatized reliver, besides being unaware of reliving, often hardly even remembers a trauma at the time of reliving it, the narrator only hints at a grim precedent that he likewise "remembered not" at the time of reliving it. The terms of his reliving, as of his flashback at Ulalume's tomb, are figurative of traumatic reliving in general. He was traumatized by his beloved's burial as if he had interred her himself on the sly by night deep in a spooky forest thick with rot. This dreamlike imagery of secret burial implies no foul play beyond the guilt and shame that normally attend trauma. Enduringly bereaved, he relives the traumatic burial through the same flight of fancy in the same ashen forest while hoping against hope to find closure through new love instead.

For all that, his experience is not wholly typical of its traumatic kind. As opposed to the fairly routine tendency to escalate a trauma in the reliving, he merely retraces his figurative traumatic steps. His sudden, shocked awareness that he has done this marks a still greater departure from the standard traumatic syndrome: consciously, relivers do not as a rule gain such awareness on their own. His blindness to his whereabouts before that climactic moment of truth situates his narration on the conscious side of reliving; unconsciously, traumatic relivers know the score from the start, for they contrive the reliving unawares. At the same time, the magical, symbol-laden imaginary landscape, as he synergistically paints it in "vocal music" with its withering leaves and funereal cypress, evokes the unconscious side of reliving.[26] Poe played both sides of the traumatic experience at once, conscious and unconscious alike, on a poetic licence.

With Poe, sound is meaning. Through its consummate, rhyme-rich sound effects, its incantatory singsong sonority hypnotically echoing itself, resonating with itself as it flows irresistibly forward along the poet's blind yet eerily familiar course, mournful *Ulalume* imparts the sense of recurrence, engulfment, and fatedness combined that is the distinctive stamp of traumatic reliving. Fittingly, it does so heedless of lexical constraints along its way. Take the second of the two lovely lines from the opening stanza: "It was night in the lonesome October/Of my most immemorial year." Little does it matter that "immemorial" means too long past to remember, which the narrator cannot properly say of the year of his revisit to the "misty mid region of Weir" in that he promptly goes on to relate this revisit, albeit in surreal terms. One apologist for this misuse of "immemorial" tried redefining the word to oblige Poe: "The narrator of the poem cannot recall something he knows it is important that he should recall."[27] But the narrator does not try to recall something important; on the contrary, his memory of something important fails him for just that one night of the revisit, and then only until the anamnesis at the climax, so on that construction "my most immemorial year" would have to mean "the year in which I had my most memorable lapse of memory", which just won't do. However loosely "immemorial" is construed in the sense of

---

[26] Poe (1848): 409.
[27] Poe (1848): 420, n. 5.

"which cannot be recalled", the narrator's "most immemorial year" containing the very sequence he is narrating would have to be one that he can remember even less than his first year of life, which won't do either. Just conceivably even logomaniacal Poe did not always know what his words or phrases meant. But the stronger indication is that he knowingly overstretched that "immemorial year" for the sufficient reason that it sounded just right. "Immemorial" is alliterative on the inside already with its redundant m's, and outwardly too in a dirge-like context thick with similarly mournful m's, o's, r's, and l's. Where he wrote "immemorial" he appears to have meant "unforgettable", which fits in beat but crucially jars in tone. The suggestion is not quite that *Ulalume* sacrifices sense to sound; rather, the sense of the words it intones lies in their sound at least as much as in their definitions. And this too accords with the poem's privileging of mood over matter, or of reverie over clarity, at the interface between conscious trauma and unconscious reliving.

The narrator's memory of Ulalume's burial does not simply slip his mind on his way to her tomb just one year later; on the contrary, he gives it the slip. For along that way, the season was autumnal from the word go. Indeed, his ruminations begin with an insistent seasonal stress: "The skies they were ashen and sober;/The leaves they were crispéd and sere;/The leaves they were withering and sere ..." He nonetheless relates of himself and his sisterly soul that "we knew not the month was October". Thus they observed the season well enough, only they avoided acknowledging it so as not to notice their anniversary reliving underway. "Our memories were treacherous and sere," the narrator soon adds—treacherous in blinding them to the telltale season while also sere like that season itself. That narrator's plural "we" comes apart only once as Psyche tries briefly to dissuade him from his headlong advance toward the "tremulous light" obscuring "the secret that lies in these wolds". She fails; the two reconverge, with Psyche subordinate; unreason has the last word, as in all matters traumatic.

Reason gets even less of a hearing with the protagonist of Herman Melville's *Moby-Dick* of 1851, a "mighty"[28] whale of a yarn for all its loose threads, bulky cetological asides, and tangled overlay of

---

[28]Melville (1851): 456: "To produce a mighty book, you must choose a mighty theme. No great and enduring volume can ever be written on the flea."

symbols and omens encumbering the stupendous saga at the heart of it. This saga is cast in the antique heroic mold of a "grand, ungodly god-like man"[29] pursuing a deadly fate "in all his fatal pride"[30] with a whole retinue in tow. Crystalline on the surface, it has depths like the oceans it sweeps in the wake of a whaling captain named Ahab as he pursues an oversized white whale nicknamed Moby Dick to the ends of the earth. Having lost a leg to Moby Dick in the south Pacific "while darting at the monster, knife in hand",[31] and fallen prey to the fixed idea of avenging his loss as "his torn body and gashed soul bled into one another"[32] on his slow voyage back home to Nantucket, "stricken Ahab"[33] takes command of a new whaling party, gains it to his frenzied cause, and, driving it for months and years even as he is driven by "his one unsleeping, ever-pacing thought",[34] runs the monster down at last "hard by the very latitude and longitude where his tormenting wound had been inflicted".[35] There he battles it anew, with the result that unlike that "gliding great demon of the seas of life",[36] its belly full of harpoons, Ahab and his whole company go under along with their fractured vessel except only the crewman-narrator buoyed up by a floating coffin.

On the face of it, Captain Ahab craves vengeance every knot of his way. His professed agenda is starkly simple: "I will dismember my dismemberer."[37] His chief mate protests this "heaven-insulting purpose"[38] to no avail, exclaiming: "Vengeance on a dumb brute! that simply smote thee from blindest instinct! Madness!"[39] Ahab, however—like many an observer or victim of Moby Dick's mischief, only more so—imputes malign cunning and "infernal aforethought of ferocity"[40] to "that mortal monster".[41] A commander of another

---

[29] Melville (1851): 79.
[30] Melville (1851): 519.
[31] Melville (1851): 184.
[32] Melville (1851): 185.
[33] Melville (1851): 124.
[34] Melville (1851): 160.
[35] Melville (1851): 536.
[36] Melville (1851): 187.
[37] Melville (1851): 168.
[38] Melville (1851): 169.
[39] Melville (1851): 163–64.
[40] Melville (1851): 183.
[41] Melville (1851): 230.

whaler who has lost an arm to Moby Dick remarks to Ahab on the high seas: "he's best let alone; don't you think so, Captain?" Wildly undeterred, blood boiling and pulse thumping, Ahab snaps back: "What is best let alone ... is not always what least allures."[42]

Ahab's rejoinder cuts to the traumatic quick. The quest for vengeance, foremost on his mind as in Melville's novel, fronts for a more malignant quest in both. Deep within, "branded Ahab"[43] is dead set not on avenging his "crucifixion"[44] at all costs, but quite the contrary on reliving it with a vengeance—on reliving it faithfully, that is, but also with the ante upped. He relives it faithfully in that he again darts the whale head-on, and again misses, right in the vicinity of their first encounter. Indeed, he thrice dislodges his false, whalebone leg in the long run-up to the replay, and then it is snapped down to "but one short sharp splinter" in a preliminary skirmish, prompting his telltale outcry: "I account no living bone of mine one jot more me, than this dead one that's lost."[45] At the same time he ups the ante in that, by way of reliving, he destroys himself together with all his shipmates save one. He religifies the catastrophe to boot in that all the world's evils since Adam, "to crazy Ahab, were visibly personified, and made practically assailable in Moby Dick".[46]

On all scores Ahab is a model reliver reliving a model trauma. The initial, traumatic blow has struck out of the blue as, "suddenly sweeping his sickle-shaped lower jaw beneath him, Moby Dick had reaped away Ahab's leg".[47] Ahab in return plans the reliving night and day down to the last particular. That, deep down, "awful Ahab"[48] is planning a reliving and not a revenge is artfully intimated by Melville through one loaded phrase after another touching the lure of what is best let alone. Witness Ahab's self-stultifying boast to himself: "steel skull, mine; the sort that needs no helmet in the most brain-battering fight!"[49] Just once, and then trenchantly, Melville passes from intimation to exposition: as Ahab lay agonizing after

[42] Melville (1851): 441.
[43] Melville (1851): 544.
[44] Melville (1851): 124.
[45] Melville (1851): 560.
[46] Melville (1851): 184.
[47] Melville (1851): 184.
[48] Melville (1851): 151.
[49] Melville (1851): 167.

he first twisted his ivory limb he "plainly seemed to see, that ... all miserable events do naturally beget their like".[50] This formulation aptly conveys the automation of traumatic reliving. So does the recurrent motif of fatedness: "This whole act's immutably decreed," cries Ahab characteristically at the finale, and again: "I am the Fates' lieutenant; I act under orders."[51] His one flash of awareness aside, Ahab's reliving was self-concealed, but reminders abound of the secret byways of "his hidden self"—of the "larger, darker, deeper part" of him "where his whole awful essence sits".[52] Melville's narrative thrives on its revealing while concealing in Ahab's own manner—on its close alignment with Ahab's own unclarity about what just once he "plainly seemed to see".

Trauma can spell guilt. Grandiose traumatized Ahab feels like Adam "staggering beneath the piled centuries since Paradise".[53] His magnified traumatic reliving, from his usurpation of the whaling expedition to the penalty in lives lost, compounds the guilt inherent in the trauma itself. Worse, he sees that magnified reliving, although terminal in this world, as the merest exponential beginning: in "the other world ... some guilty mortal miseries shall still fertilely beget to themselves an eternally progressive progeny of griefs beyond the grave".[54] Guilty or no, his traumatic woe, "completely possessing him",[55] also galvanizes him: "If such a furious trope may stand, his special lunacy stormed his general sanity, and carried it, and turned all its concentrated cannon upon its own mad mark; so that far from having lost his strength, Ahab, to that one end, did now possess a thousand fold more potency than ever he had sanely brought to bear upon any one reasonable object."[56] Above all, he acquires the uncanny power, distinctive of traumatic reliving, to bend others' wills to that one end, overriding all scruples and uncertainties. "I came here to hunt whales, not my commander's vengeance," cries his chief mate,[57] who once nearly turns a loaded musket on him,

[50] Melville (1851): 464.
[51] Melville (1851): 561.
[52] Melville (1851): 185.
[53] Melville (1851): 544.
[54] Melville (1851): 464.
[55] Melville (1851): 160.
[56] Melville (1851): 185.
[57] Melville (1851): 163.

thinking: "shall this crazed old man be tamely suffered to drag a whole ship's company down to doom with him?"[58] Yet even that mutinous mate submits, as does the entire restive "gloomy crew", whose misgivings "were fain to hide beneath their souls".[59] Melville individuates a dozen or so of the ship's ever so diverse company of thirty that Ahab succeeds in goading along. "My one cogged circle fits into all their various wheels," he gloats after first winning their compliance with the hunt for Moby Dick,[60] only to reflect: "They think me mad ... but I'm demonic, I am madness maddened!"[61] By the time of the deathly finale, his ascendancy over his men is total "whatever pale fears and forebodings some of them might have felt before".[62] Thenceforth even the plural "men" no longer quite holds, for "all the individualities of the crew, this man's valor, that man's fear; guilt and guiltlessness, all varieties were welded into oneness, and were all directed to that fatal goal which Ahab their one lord and keel did point to." Pithily put, "they were one man, not thirty".[63] Lacking a prior group identity, they represent the extreme of a traumatized leader's following fashioned by the sheer force of his prepotent drive to relive. "Ye are not other men," Ahab tells them in the final struggle, "but my arms and my legs; and so obey me."[64] At that high point, his reliving is theirs as well.

Traumatic unreason carries the day even with the sane and sober principals of Ibsen's *Rosmersholm* of 1886. This first and lengthiest of Ibsen's dramatizations of traumatic reliving is named for the stately family seat of John Rosmer, a former preacher who has lost the faith since about the time when his wife, Beate, hurled herself into a millrace some eighteen months before the on-stage action begins. Her death hit Rosmer the harder for his having wanted her out from between him and her bewitching young resident helper, Rebecca West, and he guiltily senses that she stepped, or dove, aside out of love for him. On his side of the on-stage action he induces Rebecca to take the same plunge from the same footbridge as his wife before her,

[58]Melville (1851): 514–15.
[59]Melville (1851): 536.
[60]Melville (1851): 167.
[61]Melville (1851): 168.
[62]Melville (1851): 556.
[63]Melville (1851): 557.
[64]Melville (1851): 568.

and this in order for her in turn to prove her love for him. Clinching the replay, he pronounces her his wife on the very brink. Escalating the replay, he then takes the plunge along with her. She herself had earlier programmed the replay for him when she rejected his marriage proposal with a threat to go his late wife's way if ever he renewed it. Upon duly renewing it, he elicited a muffled confession from her: she had grown up in sin with an adoptive father who had turned out to be her natural father. This confession falls into place at Rosmersholm, where after her keeper's death she had recreated their guilty ménage by assuming the role of adoptive daughter, tending Rosmer's ailing wife as she had tended her ailing father, converting Rosmer to freethinking as her father had converted her, and conducting a secret, illicit affair with Rosmer as with her father before him. She completed this re-edition of her first guilty ménage by removing Rosmer's wife from the scene. True, Rosmer, unlike her previous keeper, kept their passionate affair sexless, but she supplied the deficiency once and for all by leading his wife, who was desperately unable to conceive and crazily guilt-ridden as a result, to believe her pregnant by Rosmer. Her ruse achieved its deadly aim in vain in that afterwards her wild craving for Rosmer hit up against his phobic fixation on the fatal footbridge.[65] No matter: wild craving or no, her incestuous past ruled out sex for her anyway.[66] This realization, together with a felt need to expiate, brings her macabre mood into sync with his for the grim finale.[67]

Was Rebecca reliving a trauma on her side in recreating at Rosmersholm her precedent guilty ménage? One traumatic blow to be half expected from her earlier setup would be a sudden discovery of her incest while in the thick of it or conceivably even afterwards, but nothing she says or does at Rosmersholm so much as hints at her reliving such an earlier shock of awareness. She does panic for fear of exposure when Rosmer's prying brother-in-law grazes the truth about her adoptive father, but that does not quite argue an earlier traumatic discovery of who her bed-mate was or had been. Still less does her spontaneous confession to Rosmer and his brother-in-law of guilt in her mistress's suicide appear to recast such an earlier

[65] Ibsen (1886): 326 and 321, 322.
[66] Ibsen (1886): 322.
[67] Ibsen (1886): 326.

discovery: a displacement by her from incest to murder together with a switch from discovery to confession would lack the compelling clarity of the reliving that Ibsen crafted for Rosmer. Rebecca's guilty ménage at Rosmersholm already reflects its prototype a bit too distortedly to carry full conviction. What Rebecca relives undistortedly is her victim's fate, from the sexual deprivation that had fed Beate's hysteria through all of Beate's known last actions culminating in a self-sacrifice intended to "free" Rosmer[68] (and even including one she first learns about only after repeating it: writing to a radical newspaper editor). But is not this suicide by Rebecca, which replicates her victim's, a traumatic replay on Rebecca's side as it is on Rosmer's? Here again the traumatic impetus is lacking as the play stands. A horrific shock when her victim actually took the plunge at her prodding can perhaps be extrapolated from Rebecca's account of having struggled against herself at every step, only then she missed her cue in replying only sparsely and coldly when asked if she felt no remorse since she showed none: "That's for me to settle with myself."[69] Nor finally does her intense erotic frustration after she has cleared her way to Rosmer qualify as a trauma replayed through her later refusal to marry him: a trauma that gets relived is not a frustration that settles in slowly, but more like a blow which strikes out of the blue.

The signs point to an inchoate intention on Ibsen's part to match Rosmer's traumatic reliving with one by Rebecca on the bridge beside him even though her suicide in her predecessor's footsteps wound up scripted as more guilt-driven than trauma-driven. But Rosmer himself, it must be added, breaks the ground rules for traumatic reliving in that he, earlier along in the process than Poe's narrator in *Ulalume*, relives his trauma consciously rather than unconsciously, inviting Rebecca in so many words to assume his wife's identity ("You shall be for me the only wife I have ever had"[70]) and to do as his wife had traumatically done before her ("to go the same way—as Beate went"[71]). Conversely, it accords with an intended traumatic undertheme of the play as a whole that the two

[68]Carlson (1974): 273.
[69]Ibsen (1886): 318.
[70]Ibsen (1886): 307.
[71]Ibsen (1886): 325.

principals expressly act out a compulsion beyond their control in each case. Rebecca insists that she did not take the decision to drive Rosmer's wife to suicide, but that it took her: "It came over me like a storm at sea. ... No thought of standing against it."[72] And Rosmer gives Rebecca her final instructions for the footbridge—to quote Ibsen's redundantly emphatic stage direction—"as if involuntarily driven against his own will".[73]

Ibsen was to perfect the device of traumatic reliving theatrically in his next, and last, productive decade but, strange to say, only for use in two first acts, which each steal and hence spoil the show. In *Little Eyolf* (1894), a jealous and domineering wife has previously seduced her husband into making love to her while their infant son, left untended, took a crippling fall from a table; years afterwards they recycle, or reconfigure, this traumatic sequence in unison as they thrash out their failed moral duty toward the same, now lame, boy while he, again untended, falls from a pier outdoors and drowns. And in Ibsen's last play, *When We Dead Awaken* (1899), a sculptor's model, frustrated by his strictly artistic use of her lush naked flesh over long months, then devastated when he merely thanks her off for the happy episode, relives that unhappy episode as a strip artist exciting men only to leave them suicidally high and dry until she drives herself crazy in the process. Both plays, however, move on from the trauma relived to the sufferers' futile struggles to put it behind them. Wise old Ibsen's masterly manipulation of the mechanism of traumatic reliving, with all its symbolic subterfuges and perverse poetry, puts those two first acts high among the greatest first acts in the entire theatrical repertory. The pity is that they cannot stand alone.

So much for six disparate fictional treatments of traumatic reliving taken separately. Now, what do they say in common about this common theme?

In all six the reliving occurs as if initiated outside of the self. In *Ion* it is prompted by a slave, in *Athaliah* by a magical nightmare, in *Ulalume* occultly by Astarte; Francesca and Paolo suffer it as an imposed punishment; Ahab feels coerced by fate, Rosmer driven against his will, and Rebecca (if she counts as also reliving

[72] Ibsen (1886): 321; cf. 317–18.
[73] Ibsen (1886): 325.

on her side) blown by the likes of a storm at sea. Even so, it comes thick with reliver's guilt in every case. Traumatized Creusa feels guilty over her exposed child, Athaliah over her supposedly murdered grandchild, Rosmer over his wife's suicide on his account, and Rebecca over her incest; Ahab claims the guilt of the ages for no good reason, Francesca and Paolo are convicted sinners, and the poet-narrator in *Ulalume* hints, if only figuratively, at some unutterable transgression when, on the selfsame night a year before, he bore a "dread burden" to its secret burial. The guilt-laden reliving is agonizing in Euripides until it gets a far-fetched happy twist; for the rest, it is endlessly painful in Dante, ghastly in Poe, and fatal in Melville, Racine, and Ibsen. Apart from *Ion*, nowhere that I know in literature does traumatic reliving come to a happy end.[74] This being so, that Euripidean twist has the look of a Euripidean jest. Even with that twist, however, the reliving is no more curative in *Ion* than elsewhere. What detraumatizes Creusa is her reunion with Ion, not her failed attempt on his life. Moreover, *Ion* excepted, the common suggestion is of a self-punitive mechanism projected outwards.

In this projection outwards, as in all else, these fictional instances of traumatic reliving fit the non-fictional pattern even where they differ among themselves. As a rule, real-life traumas that get relived are pinpointed in time, like Francesca's murder, Ulalume's burial, Ahab's amputation, and Rosmer's wife's suicide. But real-life traumas that get relived can also come in instalments, like the rape and exposure in *Ion*, or Jezebel's murder and Joash's failed murder in *Athaliah*; these instalments are then conflated in the reliving the way they are in Euripides and Racine. The six traumas relived fictionally are more drastic on balance than our historic models, beginning with a brutal rape by a god. But their reliving tends to display the same features as our historic models, and in roughly the same proportions. On the other hand, one or another earmark of traumatic reliving is always dramatically highlighted in the fictional cases. Creusa fiercely overrides all decency on her blocked course of reliving. Francesca relives under a heavy-hanging unworldly constraint. Athalia relives with huge guilt and ruthlessness combined. Poe's narrator accentuates the fatedness of his way at every step. Ahab sweeps others along inhumanely like a force of nature driving him.

---

[74]It does, however, in a movie: see Almodóvar's *Todo sobre mi madre* below, 121.

And Rosmer manipulates his victim as if he were being manipulated. As to form, while Athaliah's insistence that Joash "be made to thrust the knife into my breast" on "the spot where I had him struck" is a clear-cut, classic reversal, the other fictional originals are all replayed straight. Finally, relivings are escalated about as often in these fictional samples as in real life. Thus Creusa tries mercilessly to kill grown-up Ion after having wept on exposing baby Ion; Francesca is reliving her ruptured loveless affair in perpetuity; Athaliah will perish by the knife on the very spot where Joash survived; Ahab drags practically all of his ship's company under with him; and Rosmer joins his second wife in jumping off the bridge right where his first wife jumped off it alone. On the other hand, Athaliah will die no more horrifically than her mother, and Poe's narrator merely returns to Ulalume's tomb by the same path as he had taken to bury her the year before. In sum, these traumatic relivings representative of Western drama and poetry of diverse ages are true to life by and large in all essentials as well as in the occasional formal differences from one to the next.

I suspect that their six authors never thought about trauma as such—that from Euripides to Ibsen they simply cast and recast their imaginary material until it felt real. But to feel real to its authors, fiction has required ever more psychologizing since the nineteenth century. For the foregoing Enlightenment, reliving trauma had been just one more seriocomical way of the world. Readers found it only fitting that once sudden pillage, rape, and slaughter befell the idyllic castle of Thunder-Ten-Tronckh at the start of Voltaire's *Candide* of 1759, its survivors should encounter pillage, rape, and slaughter at every turn of their later worldwide peregrinations (except, to be sure, in trauma-proof Eldorado), or that Uncle Toby in Lawrence Sterne's *Tristram Shandy* of 1767, even in laying amorous siege to the fair widow Wadman, should be forever refighting the siege of Namur at which he received a crippling wound to the groin ("not an old woman in the village or five miles round, who did not understand the difficulties of my Uncle Toby's siege").[75] As late as Nathaniel Hawthorne's "Roger Malvin's Burial" of 1846 a frontiersman might still shoot his son dead, no questions asked, on the very spot where

[75]Sterne (1767): III: 194.

he had once guiltily left his wife's father to die unburied. By contrast, psychologistic Melville and Ibsen were hardly lone pioneers in probing traumatic replay beyond their predecessors; they just outprobed their rivals. Consider Balzac's *Colonel Chabert* of 1832–1844. The title character, left for dead in a ditch on the battlefield at Eylau, reappears destitute in Paris long years later to reclaim his lost identity and a just portion of his estate. His case is solid, but his widow's grasping trickery on top of the legal tangles so revolts him that he throws up his hands, tells her: "I must go back under the ground,"[76] and winds up in a hospice refusing to answer to his name. (His lawyer remarks that Chabert had come full circle from a foundling home through Eylau to a homeless shelter.[77]) Or take Dostoyevski's *The Eternal Husband* of 1870, where a provincial official mourning his wife finds an unsent letter by her to a lover who had played him for a friend. Devastated, he drags his friend-turned-enemy to meet his intended new bride, who, duly charmed, now scoffs his suit away. Topping that off, he fondly nurses his traumatizer through a raging fever only to attack him with a razor afterwards. Or again, take Gerhart Hauptmann's novella "Rail Signal Man Thiel" of 1888 with its trauma by instalments of mounting severity. Thiel first surprises his wife abusing his child from a previous marriage. Next he has a nightmare of the boy's late mother clutching a bloody bundle beside the railroad bank. Finally a train runs the boy over when the stepmother lets him out of her sight. Crazed by the staggered blow, Thiel takes an axe to her and their own baby. In none of these three stories does the reliving display the common run of secondary features. And it is impure in all three: Chabert relives too nearly consciously, Dostoevsky's eternal husband replays the friend-to-enemy sequence as if out of ambivalence, and crazed Thiel's wife murder on top of his child murder was overkill. Yet even impure, the reliving carries each tale powerfully forward.

Pure reliving rings all the truer to readers, to judge by the broad and lasting appeal of works that turn on it such as the six masterly ones discussed above. Yet more than likely their public never thinks about traumatic reliving as such any more than their authors did, whether in regard to Creusa resolving in a rage to kill blameless

---

[76] Balzac (1832–1844): 142–45.
[77] Balzac (1832–1844): 144.

Ion, or Francesca mired in a loveless lust cut short by her murder, or tormented Athaliah setting herself up as her victim's victim, or Ulalume's bereaved lover blindly finding his way back to her crypt, or maddened Ahab out for vengeance on a dumb blubbery beast, or Rosmer grooming his wife's successor to recommit his wife's suicide. But in never thinking about traumatic reliving as such, readers or spectators accept it implicitly as a fact of life, however foreign the world of Creusa, Francesca, Athaliah, Poe's poet-narrator, Ahab, or Rosmer may be to them in other respects. Such implicit acceptance from age to age establishes the reality of traumatic reliving more securely than any clinical or even historical evidence ever could.

CHAPTER SIX

Reliving on screen

Dig around long enough anywhere in history for traumas relived and you will find some—individual traumas, collective traumas, even the two in tandem. For no obvious reason, the pickings are somewhat slimmer in creative literature, especially for collective traumas relived: under this head only Luigi Pirandello's *Six Characters in Search of an Author* comes to mind with its six parties to a family "drama", as they call it, bound together indissolubly to keep replaying it in concert. In film as well, specimens of collective traumatic reliving are in lamentably short supply by historic standards. On the other hand, individual traumatic reliving has made itself very much at home on the silver screen, and more and more so in recent years. This most popular and most commercial of the arts has provided pure personalized instances of the mechanism on the loose in its manifold guises and disguises while probing its workings ever deeper.

Movie-makers have also spawned new and newer variants of the mechanism while drawing increasingly on its vast potential as a motif of drama and melodrama, comedy and farce. They have even injected relived trauma into history as ferment[1] and comparably added a pinch of it as a flavouring to much classic fiction adapted to the screen.[2] And they have done all of this with no clear indication that they or their public regard this run of films, as I am presenting it here, in the context of a psychological syndrome being explored or even just exploited.[3] Nor by all indications are movie-makers or movie-goers, for all that exploring and exploiting, any more finely attuned to its operations than were fifth-century Athenian playwrights or playgoers. The medium itself, with its quick cuts, crosscuts, and flashbacks, is simply more hospitable than the novel or the theatre to trauma striking with an abrupt impact and to past trauma stealthily intruding on the present. It is the better attuned to reliving of whatever sort, traumatic or no, in that repetitions are instantly recognizable when conveyed visually and, more subtly, in that on-screen images are themselves repetitions of prior performances before the camera. Even so, this inherent affinity of the medium for the theme of traumatic reliving in particular appears to have borne its lush fruit spottily and somewhat belatedly, with a rapid build-up only after a whole cinematic century.

My cut-off for literary fiction before Freud infiltrated it cannot serve for the movies, since they flourished only after Freud's influence was felt worldwide. But no prejudice will result, as movies on the whole have not been theoretically self-conscious about traumatic reliving the way that so much literary fiction has been since Freud cut in on literary consciousness. Besides, the few loosely Freudian films have usually, like Freud's own case histories, probed chronic

---

[1] At a misfire extreme, Luc Besson's *The Messenger* of 1999 devised a murder-then-rape of Joan of Arc's elder sister by English soldiers before Joan's very eyes to fuel the stunning subsequent exploits of the maid-in-arms as she then gets her kicks from killing English soldiers.

[2] Thus for his 1995 adaptation of Jean Giono's *Le hussard sur le toit* (*The horseman on the roof*) Jean-Paul Rappenau had the heroine escape from cholera-infested Manosque only to gallop back on an indomitable impulse, and Tim Burton's *Sleepy Hollow* of 1999 had Washington Irving's headless horseman beheading his beheaders at the promptings of a witch who became one out of shock at his beheading.

[3] However, Pedro Almodóvar appears to have himself been the source of the account on the official website for his *Todo sobre mi madre* of its four symbolically equivalent train rides ("Manuela on the run": www.sonyclassics.com/allaboutmymother/frames.htlm), the last three of which may, then, have been intentionally crafted as relivings. On the other hand, Michael Haneke could not even understand the question when I asked him at a guest appearance at Boston's Museum of Fine Arts on 18 October 2007 whether he was aware of filming a trauma relived in *Caché*.

symptoms due to trauma rather than depicting episodic reliving.[4] Similarly, psychiatrically oriented updates of the old adage that violence breeds violence, as when a traumatized soldier comes home to beat up on his wife, do not constitute relivings unless the violence inflicted is unknowingly modelled on the violence suffered.[5] Traumatic reliving proper having flourished within the cinematic medium, my pick of films will be skewed to pure products of that medium, avoiding adapted novels or plays as a rule unless they depart substantially from the originals or unless the originals were meant to be filmed. In this context of exclusions, it bears repeating that to remember a trauma however vividly on-screen as off is not to relive it,[6] and above all that not all reliving is trauma-driven—far from it.[7] Relapse in particular isn't reliving: in movies as in real life, one may have a vocation for disaster that is not disaster-induced. Where no traumatic original is in evidence, an estranged lover on-screen who enters into serial ill-fated relationships has no more place in this chapter than does a routinely used and abused woman on-screen who keeps renewing a vain quest for true love.[8] They will not be missed; our hands will be full enough without them.

---

[4]Typically, Alfred Hitchcock's *Marnie* of 1964 traces its heroine's frigidity and thievery back to a girlhood trauma, while Michael Powell's *Peeping Tom* of 1960 and Gus Van Sant's *Good Will Hunting* of 1997 saddle their heroes respectively with voyeuristic sadism and neurotic guilt from a whole traumatic childhood.

[5]Thus in Susanne Bier's *Brødre* (*Brothers*) of 2004 a United Nations peacekeeper captured in Afghanistan is induced at gunpoint to beat a fellow captive to death; liberated and repatriated, he beats up on his wife—out of sexual jealousy, however, with no counterpart to the captivity or the gunpoint.

[6]Notable treatments of traumatic recall without reliving include Nicolas Roeg's *Wenn die Gondeln Trauer tragen* (*When gondolas wear mourning*) of 1973 and Adrian Lynne's *Jacob's Ladder* of 1990.

[7]The *locus classicus* of repetitive reliving with no trauma to back it up is Harold Ramis's *Groundhog Day* of 1993. Tom Tykwer's *Lola rennt* (*Run Lola run*) of 1998 is conversely off limits: it shows a trauma being suffered in three consecutive variants.

[8]As in Michelangelo Antonioni's *L'eclisse* (*The eclipse*) of 1962 and Federico Fellini's *Le notti di Cabiria* (*Cabiria's nights*) of 1957 respectively. This poignant Fellini comes ever so close to a traumatic reliving in that it begins when a false boyfriend pushes Cabiria into the Tiber and absconds with her purse (she almost drowns), and it ends when a false suitor leads Cabiria to the Tiber's edge and absconds with her purse even as she begs him to push her in—only *he* leads *her* there. A near miss this same way is Patrice Leconte's *Le mari de la coiffeuse* (*The hairdresser's husband*) of 1990: the hero, having grown up frequenting a buxom hairdresser who commits suicide, enjoys a ten-year honeymoon with a ravishing hairdresser until she in turn commits suicide—not by his devising, however, but for fear of his cooling off with age.

Like relapse, revenge on screen can come treacherously close to traumatic reliving or even overlap with it at the fringes. Conversely, where a trauma has been caused by an offending party, reliving it in reverse on screen or off, with a stand-in for the offending party, may look like mere vicarious revenge. More trickily still, reliving it straight, with or without a stand-in, may look and even feel like failed revenge. Paradigmatic on this last score in letters is our Captain Ahab in *Moby Dick*: ostensibly out to avenge his mutilation on his whale of an antagonist, he yet knows that deep down he is hell-bent rather on reliving it with a vengeance.

On a fine line between revenge and reliving on screen is François Truffaut's *La mariée était en noir* (*The bride wore black*) of 1968, which opens with a newlywed couple leaving a church as seen from a distant window through which one of a circle of five huntsmen sportingly shoots the groom dead. Although the five promptly disperse in order to escape detection, the widowed bride ascertains their identities, runs them all down, engages disarmingly with three of them by turns, and murders those three one by one. Just as she approaches the fourth, he is arrested, so she jumps the gun to the fifth, then confesses her run of murders to date and goes to jail, there to finish off the skipped fourth. The plot is strained from first to last—from how she ever identifies the five bloody sportsmen where the police cannot to how she could count on getting sent to the same jail as number four. What holds it all together is the sustained intensity of the traumatic compulsion that lends her extraordinary powers to inflict on each of the five a death out of the blue like the one that befell her bridegroom. But trauma or no, her sole purpose is retaliation; she is mindful of that purpose at every turn, and its accomplishment settles her emotional accounts, all of which tells against traumatic reliving.

Perhaps the ultimate in on-screen revenge encroaching on reliving is Clint Eastwood's *High Plains Drifter* of 1973, a Western about a mining town where the residents once impassively watched three hired killers lash to death the federal marshal who discovered that the town mine was on government property. Buried in an unmarked grave, the victim nonetheless returns unrecognized with such heightened fire power that the townsmen engage him to defend them against those same three killers due back in deadly fury from a spell in jail. When the three arrive, guns loaded, he ducks out long enough to let them shoot the town up after all, then picks the three off by turns and rides away into the night after telling one of the surviving, mystified townsfolk: "You know my name." His is the very model of traumatic reliving up to a point. He carries his narrow intensity of purpose to a pedantic extreme, ruling out all mitigating considerations more cold-bloodedly than even Truffaut's bride in mourning. But his single purpose, like hers, is retaliatory and, once attained, spells closure. Where revenge is taken, scores are evened and usually, as with Clint Eastwood's drifter, over-evened, an eye for an eye and then some. Reliving proper may raise the traumatic stakes quite as readily as revenge; unlike revenge, however, it is always unwitting and never over and done with.

Revenge and reliving keep mixing uneasily on screen year in, year out. Typically betwixt and between is Neil Jordan's *The Brave One* of 2007. Its heroine cannot get over a brutal assault on her boyfriend and herself that takes his life. With an illicitly acquired handgun she kills first in self-defence, next after passively provoking her assailants, then after affronting a deadly bully outright, and fourthly in an act of overt aggression that closely replicates her trauma in reverse. Only she tops off this stage-wise build-up to a put-up reliving by switching to straight revenge next as she tracks and guns down her original aggressors at the finale. The two motifs, although each starkly dramatized, fail to blend here as they did at Clint Eastwood's crafty hands in *High Plains Drifter*—or again, unambiguously this time, in Clint Eastwood's *Gran Torino* of 2008, where a Korean War veteran avenges a rape by an Asian street gang even as he relives a war trauma in reverse by provoking the gang to massacre him unarmed.

The trauma-haunted widow in François Ozon's *Sous le sable* (*Beneath the sand*) of 2001 provides a final, crucial advisory. So hard hit is she by her husband's disappearance at the seashore one bright day that she hallucinates his continuing presence in her daily life. When, after some months, his horrendously decomposed body is fished out of the sea, she insists on viewing it despite the mortician's strong forewarning. Hard hit anew, she denies that the wristwatch found on the body was her husband's and resumes her hallucinating. Considered in isolation, her insistence on viewing her husband's ghastly remains is like a deliberate, if inverted, retake on his traumatic disappearance, complete with the same reaction of obstinate denial. Yet it comes instructively short of reliving, as none of her behaviour runs to form otherwise. Constantly hallucinating her dead husband's presence, she is constantly mindful of his traumatic disappearance. Nor does she herself contrive the recovery of his body; indeed, her insistence on viewing it, after an uneasy delay, comes across not as a re-experience of his death, but as a failed effort to accept it. Finally, she exhibits no intense purposiveness, sense of fatality, or other common indicator of an inner process of reliving. In sum, the mere formal replication of a trauma does not constitute a reliving without the subjective experience of it to match.

Within my patchy cinematic compass, traumatic reliving pure entered film history as an accessory theme of a French classic of 1939: Julien Duvivier's moving tale of a theatrical retirement home, *La fin du jour* (*The end of the day*). There two aging actors, Marny and Saint-Clair, meet up thirty years after Marny's wife, Simone, died while on an escapade with Saint-Clair. Saint-Clair called the death accidental; Marny suspected suicide. Upon their reunion Saint-Clair again swears to the long-tormented widower, albeit a bit shiftily, that Simone's death was indeed an accident. At the same time, however, he captivates a young waitress close to Marny and, calling her Simone, starts leading her in turn to suicide. Marny foils this reliving just in time even as Saint-Clair goes mad in trance-like exaltation. The indication is that Saint-Clair too had been traumatized by Simone's suicide as had Marny. While Marny brooded over it, however, Saint-Clair had cavalierly put it aside behind his philanderer's façade, only to relive it under the suggestive effect of a fortuitous reunion with a Marny again affectionately attached to a young woman. Saint-Clair's reliving is thus set up for him, with no need for the usual single-minded contriving to replicate the traumatic original. Similarly, Saint-Clair acquires only half the characteristic trauma-induced power of enlisting others in his reliving: he engages the lovely waitress effortlessly, but Marny balks. Still in all, he does re-stage the traumatic event with theatrical aplomb and does duly override all scruples in the process. On balance, traumatic reliving in film was off to an auspicious start, however tardy.

Within my same patchy cinematic compass, traumatic reliving first took centre screen with Orson Welles's *A Touch of Evil*, released in 1958. In this epochal film noir, a Texan police captain has been framing killers ever since his days as a rookie cop thirty years before, when his wife was first assaulted, then strangled with one of her stockings, by a Mexican "half-breed" who, although apprehended, went free for lack of evidence: "I followed around after him ..." the traumatized captain explains, "ate my heart out trying to catch him, but I never did. ... That was the last killer that ever got out of my hands." Now, while investigating the murder of an American at a Texan border crossing, he helps a Mexican lowlife get a young wife gang-assaulted only to strangle him afterwards with one of her stockings beside her tortured body. His associate later suggests: "Drunk and crazy as you must have been when you strangled him, I guess you were somehow thinking of your wife, the way she was strangled." The captain more than agrees: "Always thinking of her, drunk or sober." On the surface of this reliving, the assaulted young wife out of the original trauma was recast straight in the replay as an assaulted young wife, but the original "half-breed" assailant and murderer was split two ways: into a Mexican assailant and the Texan captain-murderer. On the Texan side of this split, vicarious revenge mixes into the reliving as a by-motive. Even so, that reliving was complete in the final tally—felt guilt inclusive, the policeman-strangler having left his incriminating cane on the scene of his crime.

Another classic film noir, Roman Polanski's *Chinatown* of 1974, transmuted the brutal traumatic theme of *A Touch of Evil* into veritable traumatic poetry at its protagonist's expense. Long before the on-screen action begins, that protagonist had been a cop in Los Angeles' Chinatown when, as he guilelessly and guiltily relates, "I was trying to keep someone from being hurt. I ended up making sure that she was hurt." After this traumatic misadventure he had quit the police force, scarred for life. Unable to "find himself", he has by the movie's start refashioned himself instead into a cocky, rash private detective. A local potentate hires him to locate a missing girl and warns him: "You may think you know what you're dealing with, but believe me, you don't." He replies: "That's what the district attorney used to tell me in Chinatown." Again he collapses those two time frames, past and present, when he observes to his client's daughter, just widowed and at once haughty and frightened, that in Chinatown "you can't always tell what's going on—like with you". Failing to take his own hint, he undertakes to keep this second someone, whom he now loves in her turn, from being hurt in her turn ("I don't want to hurt you," he tells her forebodingly) even while again making sure that she is hurt. Just when he has her safely hiding in Chinatown with the missing girl he was hired to find—her sister and daughter both, fathered by her own father, who now covets the girl next—he foolhardily goes alone to his powerful, rapacious, incestuous client to claim his fee for locating the girl and vaunt his proof that the dread tycoon murdered his daughter's husband while massively swindling the city for years. Predictably, that high and mighty low-life's gunman forces him to lead them to the daughter's and granddaughter's hideaway. Up to that point Chinatown had been repeatedly evoked as an unseen, murky-mysterious presence in the inner recesses of the city, at once site and symbol of the unseen, murky-mysterious trauma haunting the inner recesses of the detective's mind. The town within a town comes into open view at last for the tragic finale. After the ill-fated fugitive wounds her father and drives off with their daughter, the police shoot her dead on her father's orders at the wheel of her getaway van. With the camera then slowly receding, the sight and sound of the vehicle are gradually swallowed up into Chinatown, and Chinatown into the measureless urban sprawl. The protagonist's defining trauma has been relived no less completely for having, like Chinatown, been intimated only in barest outline.

Beyond traumatic reliving *Chinatown* evokes, with the same blend of naturalism and symbolism, a broad spectrum of the public and private corruption endemic to modern life in the canons of film noir. By dizzying contrast, Alfred Hitchcock's 1958 thriller *Vertigo* focuses sharply throughout on a guilty fear of heights dominating its hero's sick soul. Around that fear the action nominally turns. Scottie, a San Francisco cop, slips on a chase across some rooftops and winds up clutching a flimsy gutter dizzyingly high above ground even as a colleague who tries to rescue him goes crashing down. Scottie somehow survives, but after a stretch of failed therapy he quits the force while still spinning with vertigo and groaning with guilt. A former college classmate with a wealthy, unwanted wife, Madeleine, and a gorgeous girlfriend, Judy, hires him to keep a private eye on Madeleine impersonated by Judy and pretendedly self-identified with a grandmother who committed suicide.

To authenticate her act, the pseudo-Madeleine jumps into the Bay. Scottie fishes her out, takes her home, and easily falls in love with her while her clothes are drying nearby. But when she climbs the bell tower from which her alleged grandmother took a fatal leap he foreseeably cannot follow the whole way up. He hears her scream, glimpses a woman in free fall, and supposes it to be Madeleine—as indeed it is, only this time the real Madeleine, her neck fresh-broken beforehand. Crazed with new and worse grief and traumatic guilt commingled, Scottie does another futile stint in a mental ward, then aimlessly wanders the streets, moping. One day he runs into Judy, now a shop girl with her pre-Madeleine looks and manner: she had been only paid off for playing Madeleine. They take up again, with her denying any knowledge of the late Madeleine in whose image he peskily insists on remaking her. But one evening he recognizes a necklace of Madeleine's on her, divines the truth, and forces her and himself together up the death tower, claiming to want her confession there so as to clear the air: "When it's done we'll both be free," he tells her. But then his ominous last words to her are: "Too late. It's too late. There's no bringing her back." By then he has so taunted and rattled her that, at the sudden sight of a nun drawn by their voices, she spins off the tower down into the void like dead Madeleine before her. Whereas Scottie at the tower was ostensibly out to purge himself of his guilt-drenched Madeleine trauma, declaring: "I want to stop being haunted," he actually relived that trauma instead with singular, uncanny literalness in driving a Judy refashioned as Madeleine to commit Madeleine's supposed suicide, this time for real. To parallel, two-tier effect, the film foregrounds Scottie's vertigo from first to last, although with the traumatic reliving poking out from behind. Of the earmarks of traumatic reliving, guilt looms largest in this case, with narrow intensity of purpose running a close second and a climactic traumatic escalation bringing up the rear. So compellingly is Scottie's psychological mishmash conveyed, including his wrenching ambivalence toward Judy at the end, that the utter preposterousness of the plot gets lost from sight. Nor was that preposterousness the scenarist's failing; rather (as in Ibsen's *Rosmersholm*, only more so), it was the price of a death trauma replayed live.

As against film noir with its mix of motifs and Hitchcock's Scottie with his mix of motives, the first filming of a traumatic reliving in total thematic isolation that I know[9] was Satyajit Ray's bare-bones archetypal *Jalsaghar* (*The Music Room*) of 1958, the same charmed year as Welles's *A Touch of Evil* and Hitchcock's *Vertigo*.[10] In Ray's fable-like, dreamlike drama, the master of a musty Bengal mansion remembers how he once took his wife's jewels from their house safe to throw an extravagant coming-of-age party for their son in their stately music room and how afterwards his wife set out with the new adult to visit her parental family across an adjacent lake: their bark capsized in a storm and washed ashore empty. Now years later, when the aged, broken master of the neglected mansion is invited to a similar coming-of-age party for the son of a newly rich neighbour, he objects impulsively that he himself intended throwing a party on that very same date in memory of his own late son. Stirred into action, he removes his last rupees from the house safe where his wife's jewels had lain beside them, refurbishes the music room that has been shut since the double drowning, and excitedly holds a repeat performance of the original grand concert and reception. When this duplicate soirée ends, he rides in frenzy straight to the lakeside, where his horse bolts at the bark, untouched since the traumatic event, and throws him to his death. This replay is as parsimonious and pointed as replays come: his own death beside the bark has doubled for his wife's and son's. It is ushered in visually by a second shot of the house safe being emptied of the second half of its contents. The fatality ahead is forecast in effect when his one remaining servant reminds him that those rupees are his last. In the throes of reliving, he has no more thought to spare for that servant's welfare or his own after his splurge than he had qualms about telling his yuppie neighbour the lie that he had long since planned a memorial party for that same date. True to type, the replay re-energizes him electrically: after long years of lethargic brooding he enlists teams of workmen and then a roomful of guests in his sudden enterprise. A characteristic traumatic mood of doom hangs

---

[9]Michael Curtiz's iconic *Casablanca* of 1943 may look like an earlier specimen in that the heroine first breaks off a love affair on her husband's account, then her traumatized lover breaks it off himself on her husband's account when fate returns her to his arms. In each case, however, the intended reason is the husband's role in the anti-Nazi underground.

[10]To be exact, *A Touch of Evil* was released that year but shot earlier.

heavy over the forced gaiety of the long-drawn-out, déjà-vu musical evening. The overall effect is so compelling that the single weak note of the classic traumatic score can pass unnoticed: the need for a neighbour's invitation to touch off that frenzied bout of reliving. Or is that need truly a weakness?

Either way, no such note is struck by another archetypal traumatic reliving, one screened nearly half a century later and not merely fable-*like*, as in *Jalsaghar*, but pure fable. In the third episode of George Lucas's *Star Wars*, subtitled *Revenge of the Sith* and dated 2005, the dominant figure of the series is obsessed by his mother's death in agony. He accordingly gets his secret wife with child only to suffer from a nightmare of her too dying in agony upon becoming a mother in her turn. Haunted but undaunted, he enters the service of the Supreme Chancellor on the dark side of the Force with the aim of gaining occult savvy to prevent his nightmare from coming true. His wife discovers his new allegiance and recoils in horror; he strikes her; she delivers prematurely, overcome by shock, and then dies in agony, whereupon he tells himself that he did everything to prevent just that dreaded outcome—the traumatic formula in its generic form. Active rather than (like Saint-Clair or the master of the Bengal mansion) reactive, he has conceived and conducted his reliving all on his own, with no suggestive input from circumstances, plying others to his traumatic project the whole way. True to form in reliving, he spectacularly espouses evil and brutally overrides his once tender love for his wife. He signals his new departure by changing his name on coming to lead the evil Empire—from Anakin Skywalker to Darth Vader. Outdoing even real-life Bismarck, who, as leader of the German empire, cast his nightmare on a mere European scale, Darth Vader escalates his cosmically in that the fate of the galaxies hinges on his switched allegiance. In this stellar extravaganza, the traumatic measure is full.

It is fully as full in Louis Malle's earthier *Damage* of 1992.[11] The titular damage is that done to a teenage girl when her jealous elder brother slits his wrists because she locks him out of her room one night after a rival has kissed her. Years later she takes up with a bigwig

---

[11] The film closely follows a 1991 novel of that name by Josephine Hart that she styled for filming by, as she hoped, Louis Malle.

politician's son reminiscent of her lost brother and, behind the son's back, with the bigwig politician himself as well. She gets engaged to the son only to keep on mating with the father anywhere, anytime, in ever more heedless heat. Typically she runs to him from the son's arms once for a quickie behind a church door. Wholly under her erotic sway—"I can't see past you," he tells her—he pleads to regularize their situation, whereas she stands firm on the explosive, quasi-incestuous arrangement. Even after he spots his daughter watching him sneak out of the fiancée's room by night at the son's engagement party he can't stop. He does once manage to call it off on her mother's urgent advice but readily relapses when she sends him the key to a secret apartment. Catastrophe, after having hung heavy for over an hour's screen time, finally strikes on the very eve of the planned wedding as she carelessly betrays her tryst nest to her bridegroom and, reversing her trauma, leaves the door unlocked, with the key dangling outside for bad measure. Her betrothed duly surprises her there panting and throbbing in unison with his father. Devastated, he falls backwards over a stairwell banister to his death. The father's career and life are ruined, but never mind: her reliving completed, the fatal lady cuts off the shattered ex-lover without a word and, closing the evil circle, marries his traumatic original, her lost brother's rival, whom she had been keeping on hold in the shadows. Her reliving was marked by telltale compulsiveness, coerciveness, and ruthlessness, together with surrender to fate and even a smattering of guilt, all the way to its escalated dénouement. Having some introspective inkling of what she is up to with the hapless father, she bares her suppurating traumatic wound to him early along and even warns him: "Remember, damaged people are dangerous"—forthrightly but, as she well knows, ineffectually. Irresistible and frightening while trauma-driven, she sinks into banality afterwards.

Equally forthcoming about the trauma that he will relive is a juvenile delinquent in André Téchiné's *Les égarés* (*Astray*) of 2003. Having escaped from a reformatory with his only friend, who then hanged himself when recaptured, he comes far enough out of hiding during the German invasion of 1940 to fend for a mother and her two sons in flight from Paris. Gradually he wins the mother's love only to get caught stealing food for her and, locked back up, to hang himself in turn. Like the vertigo in *Vertigo*, the foregrounded drama of a truncated family adrift in the massive exodus of June 1940 from Paris screens the reliving that holds the action together.

Traumatic reliving was turned inside out by Christopher Nolan's enigmatic *Memento* of 2000 about an insurance adjuster named Leonard who has caught and killed a junkie housebreaker raping and murdering his wife. His memory is stuck on this "incident", as he calls it, and can retain nothing else more than momentarily as he seeks to run down and kill a supposed second rapist. A sleazy cop manipulates him into targeting a nasty pusher loaded with cash. So does that pusher's battered and vengeful girlfriend. The plot thickens when it emerges that a short-term memory loss like his own was the basis of an insurance claim that he had guiltily disallowed just before the traumatic incident because, as in his own case afterwards, the impairment was not physical. In retrospect he imagines for the claimant a diabetic wife who, to prove his affliction authentic, has him repeat her insulin injection every few minutes until she dies. The strongest suggestion is incongruous: that Leonard had fatally overdosed his wife with insulin for her diabetes at the time of the traumatic event. To assist himself in reliving, Leonard once hires a hooker to scream for help from the next room while he sleeps: "Whatever kicks you off," she says obligingly. Any take on this slippery thriller may be questioned except Leonard's trauma itself, his fixation on it, and his relentless drive to relive it. The effect of a traumatic hang-up and reliving is only the more compelling with the trauma remaining encoded in its own idiom and hence as elusive to the spectator as to Leonard himself. The traumatic shock is ingeniously rendered as a blow to Leonard's head from an imagined duplicate rapist. His fixation on it is conveyed in the form of the memory block that makes it ever-actual, crowding out current happenings almost as they unfold. The reliving, finally, is depicted through a bagful of mutually reinforcing cinematographic tricks, including scenes repeated in reverse and the alternation of black-and-white with colour, to keep relating his perceptual present to his traumatic past. A deft flashback of pre-trauma Leonard denying the insurance claim with businesslike urbanity lends full relief to the naked, frenzied reliving that he personifies.

Memento gave both high-voltage melodrama and episodic reliving a novel on-screen twist by refracting its protagonist's story through his traumatized mind. But ever since *A Touch of Evil*, melodrama has bought heavily into traumatic reliving within the conventional rules of filmic narration as well. An exemplary specimen is Coline Serreau's *Chaos* of 2002. It begins with an Algerian teenager fleeing her family upon discovering that her father is surreptitiously selling her into marriage to a much older man. Adrift in Marseille, she gets caught up in a prostitution ring. After a desperate and unsuccessful attempt to break free, she comes into her own by cultivating the fine art of bilking affluent elderly clients out of their fortunes. This neat reliving of her engagement trauma in near-total reverse (she herself now profits from double-dealing in non-marriage to older men) comes with all the familiar signs of the syndrome: new motivation, new effectiveness, and new unscrupulousness; higher stakes than in her father's petty, foiled transaction; a heavy-hanging mood of entrapment by fate. Her reliving is offset by a countervailing case of constant traumatic recall. Once early along she tries to escape the ring and, pursued by her pimp squad, reaches out to a passing car for help; even as she is being manhandled on the street, the driver speeds off with his wife beside him; afterwards the wife is plagued by the guilty memory until she succeeds in running the battered captive down and helping her make the break after all. This object lesson in alternative traumatic after-effects is hardly less plausible for its happy outcome.

More ambitious but less successful than this juxtaposition of two different reactions to trauma is the two-sided traumatic reliving with double role reversal in Robert Berry's melodrama of 2005, *La boîte noire* (*The black box*). A traumatic bang kicks off the action as a car hits a cyclist on a seaside cliff and flips over. For some days the driver, hospitalized, lies muttering in a coma. When he comes to, a nurse gives him a tape of his mutterings, which he sorts out and checks out detective-style. They mainly bear on a fateful childhood accident. He had been peddling his younger brother when an auto struck their bicycle at that selfsame steep seaside cliff. He had survived, if badly shaken, but his brother, hurled over the edge, desperately clutched a branch for some moments before falling to his death into the rocky sea below. A neurologist from his hospital eventually points him back to the scene of the original and the repeat accident, awaits him there, unmasks himself as the driver of that first, deadly car who might have hoisted the boy to safety but then plunges off the cliff in his turn. This fatal plunge closes out the double reliving after twenty years of nagging guilt on both sides. The erstwhile big brother cyclist having played the part of the erstwhile deadly driver in replicating the accident, the erstwhile deadly driver played the role of his erstwhile victim in taking the plunge. In a deft directorial touch, the big brother's reliving in the opening sequence is shown from his vantage point as driver, so that his camera eye completes his reliving by simply letting his victim on the bicycle drop from sight. For the rest, the film is rife with implausibilities and replete with extraneous, gratuitous sex and violence, so that the two convergent, guilt-driven traumatic relivings have all they can do to carry the viewer through.

If traumatic reliving is always guilt-driven—and isn't reliving a trauma *ipso facto* self-punitive?—cinema has not much stressed the point outside of *Vertigo* and *La boîte noire* even where it has depicted the process straight. Yet it has ruled out guilt only once that I know. Saint-Clair's strong guilt over Simone's suicide is at least implicit in *La fin du jour*; the inspector in *A Touch of Evil* incriminates himself in reliving, and the one in *Chinatown* airs his guilty conscience outright; guilt is suggested in *Jalsaghar* when the master of the mansion blows his wife's jewels to fund their son's disastrous coming-of-age party; in *Star Wars: Revenge of the Sith* the son blames himself for having been unable to prevent his mother's painful death; the damage in *Damage* from a brother's suicide out of incestuous jealousy can hardly have felt fault-free; the insulin sequence in *Memento*, whatever else it may signify, does intimate guilt on Leonard's part for his wife's death in that the amnesiac who overdoses his wife is self-identified by Leonard; finally, guilt may at least be conjectured in an Algerian girl who, as in *Chaos*, flaunts her father's will and winds up a whore. On the other hand, not a trace of traumatic guilt can be detected or even imagined in the woe-begone anti-hero of Arthus de Penguern's ever so droll *Grégoire Moulin contre l'humanité* (*Grégoire Moulin versus humanity*) of 2001, a supreme cinematic specimen of traumatic reliving as farce. A scrapping couple hurl each other out of a window to their death, leaving their newborn Grégoire dumbfounded and aghast in his cradle. As a result, grown-up Grégoire manages in all innocence to keep touching off deadly aggression all around him. Grégoire is a misfit precisely by reason of his inveterate innocence: he winds up exiling himself to the moon, but only after a hilarious climax that dots the three i's and crosses the two t's of traumatic reliving as a quick, subliminal flashback to Grégoire's cradle trauma is slipped into a bloody shoot-out raging all around him on a Parisian square.

Group traumatic reliving on its side has been a relative rarity on screens the world over since its mystifying début in Luis Buñuel's *El ángel exterminador* (*The angel of death*) of 1962. In this modern-day fable, the dinner guests in a Mexico City mansion are unable to leave for weeks on end while they puzzle and squabble over their plight day and night. Then all at once they find themselves in the same seats at table as when they came and unblock themselves by repeating their first words and gestures as of that initial dinner together. Jubilant, they troop to a nearby church to give thanks—and again they can't leave. They troop there as a human herd, followed by a flock of sheep like those eaten by them some days earlier in the mansion. While their being stuck in the church pointedly throws back to their traumatic ordeal in the mansion, Buñuel does not illuminate the logic or illogic of this throwback: the church sequence is all too brief. More confusingly, he has them originally stuck in the mansion by dint of no outer constraint, but of a shared inner inhibition, as if they were already reliving an earlier group trauma, whereas they first form into a group, or herd, through their shared predicament in the mansion. Still more bafflingly, no sooner do they begin arriving for that fateful dinner than the servants start to leave as if in anticipation of the trouble ahead: apparently the baleful traumatic spell is in the air from the get-go. Repetition is the dominant mode of the film, what with images, gestures, dialogue, and even whole scenes being replayed continually. And the theme of trauma is sounded outright early along when the dinner party bind reminds one of the trapped guests of a deadly train accident that she once survived. Buñuel plainly knew what his subject was even if his surrealism dispensed him from making clear sense of it.

For its part, the clearer cinematic sense made of group traumatic reliving by M. Night Shyamalan's *The Village* of 2004 verges on nonsense. There a handful of trauma victims have opted out of today's ugly world to live together in hermetic seclusion deep inside a wildlife preserve. Their leader keeps the records of their ghastly prior ordeals locked up in a communal safe box. Fixated on the past, the villagers dress, speak, and act as if in an ancestral American settlement while teaching their children that the surrounding forest is infested with monsters who, although fierce and fearful, will do them no harm if ignored. To lend this tall tale credibility, the village elders take turns haunting the forest. But one day a young madcap discovers his father's monster costume, whereupon the skinned carcasses of animals start appearing on the forest's edge. Later it emerges from the safe box that in days of yore the village elders had each likewise seen loved ones viciously abused and slaughtered, then dumped naked like garbage; although how the madcap knew of these secreted traumatic originals is never divulged. The village bond comes loose when the chief's blind daughter gropes her way through the forest with his reluctant blessing to fetch up-to-date medication for her suitor stabbed to near death by the fake bogeyman, who perishes as she passes. The overall suggestion is of a parable of traumas pooled and repressed together in the guise of monsters held at bay ("those we do not speak of") while also being relived together chronically through the haunted forest and then also episodically through the skinned carcasses. On the down side thematically, group traumas are not individual traumas pooled, while on the up side, episodic traumatic reliving does resemble a madcap's antics.

Perhaps *El ángel exterminador* and *The Village* can more fairly be seen as imaginative variations on the theme of traumatic reliving than as flawed attempts to show the mechanism operating at the group level. To play free and loose with patterns of reliving has in fact been as much the rule as the exception in film, audiences being ever ready to suspend disbelief and buy into clever departures from the norm.

In the earliest such departure I can cite, the variant reliving was even less central to the action than was straight reliving when it debuted a few years earlier in *La fin du jour*.[12] That sidelined pseudo-reliving occurs in *Le corbeau* (*The crow*), Henri-Georges Clouzot's grim masterpiece of 1943 about poison-pen letters circulating in a French village. There a big-time big-city surgeon who lost his wife in childbirth to an obstetrician's failed attempt to save the child has remade himself into a small-time small-town obstetrician who

[12] A still earlier specimen if it counts as one is William Dieterle's *Portrait of Jenny* of 1939: see below, p. 123.

keeps delivering children dead with the mothers surviving. Thus he routinely rectifies his trauma on the mother's side while repeating it on the child's. Rectification, although often the conscious aim of unconscious reliving, is never its practical outcome. No matter: in this intense drama of dirty secrets, how authentically the ex-surgeon relives his trauma is of no more moment than how unaccountably the hapless village obstetrician stays in business. At least the cinematic mode of variations on traumatic reliving was not stillborn even if that same traumatized ex-surgeon did bring it into the world.

Except that "poetically fanciful" sounds disparaging, it would aptly describe the variation on traumatic reliving that, in Alain Resnais's *Hiroshima mon amour* (*Hiroshima my love*) of 1959, enshrined the whole theme of remembrance and recurrence in the cinematic repertoire. The scenario by Marguerite Duras (with input from Resnais) centres on a French movie actress who had loved a German soldier in her youth in Nevers under the Occupation during World War II. At the Liberation her lover was shot before her eyes, her head was shaved, and her parents hid her in their cellar out of shame. Once her hair grew back she was sneaked off to Paris, arriving just when Hiroshima was atom-bombed. Now, fifteen years later, she is acting on location in Hiroshima, beset by flashes of her personal trauma and the Hiroshima trauma intermixed—"as if," the scenarist explained, "the disaster of a woman's shaved head in Nevers exactly matched the disaster of Hiroshima".[13] On her last day she takes and retakes a Japanese lover while telling him over and over that she will forget him, that she is already forgetting him. Nameless, the two bed- and soul-mates call each other "Hiroshima" and "Nevers" as they invoke the two cities and two traumas interchangeably. With its frequent arty cuts and flashbacks mimicking traumatic recoil and recall, and its dreamy diction blending anguish and reverie, *Hiroshima mon amour* set a whole new cinematic style for conveying memories relived. It also played by the straight rules of traumatic reliving up to a point. A Japanese lover was a fit surrogate for a French woman's German lover of World War II, just as the collective trauma of Hiroshima was an apt symbolic substitute for her personal trauma marking the war's end. Those two proxies are meaningful to

[13]Duras (1960): 9–10.

her not in their own right, moreover, but only in serving her felt need to relive: so far, so fair. The unrealism begins with her knowing and saying that she is reliving: real reliving is perforce unknowing. And that unrealism is clinched by her selectiveness in reliving: although she will lose her surrogate enemy lover again and again (after enjoying him again and again), neither will he be shot nor she be shamed. But then, the very point of inventive variants is to invent and vary.

Jonathan Demme's *The Silence of the Lambs* of 1991, based on Thomas Harris's 1988 novel of the same name, overlaps with *Hiroshima mon amour* in its heroine's consciousness of her reliving. A female FBI trainee, she is assigned to sound out a jailed cannibalistic psychiatrist for leads to a former patient of his who is sewing himself a suit from women's skins and starving a new captive in order to loosen her skin before the kill. The psychiatrist exchanges hints at this woman-flayer's identity and whereabouts for intimate self-disclosures from the zealous trainee, who in the process gradually connects her current "rescue fantasy" back to a girlhood trauma. Orphaned at age ten, she was taken to live on a cousin's ranch, where she was awakened one night by the bleating of lambs slated for slaughter; she fled in distress with one of the lambs in her arms, as if to save them all by saving that one; caught and sent to an orphanage, she has inwardly heard the lambs bleating ever since. As lambs are slaughtered for their meat and their wool both, her task to track a flayer of human skin through an eater of human flesh in order to rescue a human captive slated to die is custom-made to reactivate her poignant trauma. If she does not herself contrive to relive it, she is no less driven in reliving it by her guilt over the lambs she could not save. She could not rectify its vicarious outcome and silence the lambs inside her by the straight rules of reliving. She does so instead by trading her newfound awareness of this motivation for leads to the serial killer's hideaway.[14]

At a still further remove from those who contrive and conduct their relivings with no help from propitious circumstances is Aunt Line in Claude Chabrol's *La fleur du mal* (*The flower of evil*) of 2003, who relives the trauma of her life by proxy, with little material input

---

[14] In the novel, the serial killer would undo his mother's abandonment of him in childhood by assuming her bodily identity through the "woman suit" he is sewing. The film wisely confined itself to the episodic reliving of the lamb trauma.

of her own. Under the Occupation she had murdered her hated father, a Vichy official who relished having members of the Resistance shot including his own son, her passionately beloved brother François. Charged with the parricide at the time but cleared for lack of proof, she has burned ever since with the reverse of remorse: a nagging sense of unfinished business. As she puts it, "For sixty years I've been waiting." Then a great-niece of hers with a passionately beloved stepbrother named François accidentally kills her own hated stepfather, François's father, while fending off his drunken advances. Answering her cry for help, an ecstatic Aunt Line claims the killing as her own over the girl's feeble protests and insists on their lugging the corpse upstairs to her murder room of sixty years before. Out of her traumatic depths she declares: "I feel like I'm going back and redoing things," and again: "Time doesn't exist, it's a perpetual present."[15] Second-hand though her reliving was, she did wrest it from the real killer and did cast honesty to the winds for its sake. She also stretched it just a little in assimilating a stepbrother and a stepfather to a real brother and real father and in substituting a killing in self-defence for a bona fide murder. Curiously, reviewers tended to stretch it the same way and, despite all Aunt Line's explanations, construe the titular "flower of evil" as a crime prompted by a family curse.

Nor is the reliving by the simpleminded, pious heroine of Lars von Trier's *Breaking the Waves* of 1996 authentically hers either. A blushing bride at the outset, she takes to conjugal sex with such holy relish that she can't bear her husband's absences working on an oil rig and prays for his definitive return. He does return definitively, but paralyzed and, more to the point, emasculated by an injury on the job. His lustily loving wife is traumatized with guilt to spare, given her prior prayer. "What happened on the rig was my fault," she tells God. Faithful at first, she eventually relives her side of the unsexing trauma fatally escalated in reverse by having compulsive, painful sex with strangers until she deliberately gets mutilated to death by a pair of sadists. Typical as reversal and escalation may be, she embarks on that course only at her husband's behest: to keep him alive, he insists, she must continually have sex with other men in his stead and tell him all

---

[15]This last traumatic *cri de coeur* recalls the traumatized Mother's insistence in Pirandello's *Six Characters in Search of an Author* that "it's happening now, it's happening always".

about it afterwards. Still her reliving only half qualifies as a variant; she goes on driving herself erotically after her husband can no longer hear her reports—indeed, even after he signs a warrant to have her committed because of warnings from all sides that she is destroying herself on his psychopathic account. The traumatic reliving is actually explicit to the extent that the medical finding of her cause of death is sexual perversion due to the trauma of her husband's injury, and this with no suggestion that the perversion was his to start.

A delightfully inventive variant of traumatic reliving in the form of juvenile science fiction is the first and key episode, dated 2002, of Sam Raimi's *Spider-Man*, loosely based on a comic strip of that name. In it a college boy cannot forgive himself for letting a thief rush past him who then, to steal a getaway car, kills the boy's beloved uncle waiting at the wheel to drive him home. Thereafter the lad uses mysterious on-again, off-again spider-like super powers, gained earlier from a spider bite, to forestall criminal assaults reminiscent of the one he traumatically let pass. His nagging felt guilt, preternatural empowerment, and sense of a binding vocation run to type. Conversely, while vehicular rescues predominate, his exploits occasionally leave his uncle trauma behind, such as saving a girl trapped in a burning building. All of them end happily besides, so they are more like preventions or corrections than relivings. In their puerile extravagance they would be truer to life as the boy's fantasy play—and may indeed have been meant as such, for in one scene the occasional spider-man is shown talking, unmasked, to a doctor about his dreams of being Spider-Man.

More sophisticated science fiction is Michel Gondry's *The Eternal Sunshine of the Spotless Mind* of 2004. Its hero, in the traumatic aftermath of a break-up with his girlfriend, undertakes to have every memory of her surgically erased from his brain, proceeding backwards. From one erasure to the next, however, he recovers ever more of his old love for her until in the end he refuses to complete the process. He thereby in effect revives their ill-starred romance at its take-off point, with its future course of heartbreak foreshadowed. Gorgeously conveyed, his ultimate recovery of his lost love within him in all its foredoomed depth and fullness is wholly compelling on its plane of dreamlike enchantment. It nonetheless comes short of traumatic reliving proper in that it happens subjectively only and is unintentional at any level of consciousness.

A melodramatic variant of traumatic reliving with a novel twist is Michael Haneke's *Caché* (*Hidden*) of 2005. Like *La boîte noire* it features a two-sided trauma relived on both sides, but unlike *La boîte noire* it makes a mystery of who is behind the reliving. In it Georges Laurent, a boy of six, gets an unwanted foster brother sent to an orphanage by inducing him to kill the barnyard rooster and then blaming him for the killing. The incident revisits Georges in middle age as a nightmare in which the boy turns on him, hatchet in hand, after beheading the rooster with a profuse squirt of blood. His nightmare is triggered by unsigned, childlike drawings mailed to his house from nowhere—of a hominoid figure first, then of a beheaded rooster, each beside a profuse squirt of blood. Next come videos, first of his home, then of a modest apartment. He traces this last to his former foster brother, whom he blames for the drawings and films in an ugly tirade: a videotape of it follows him home. Invited back, he returns only to see the unfortunate slit his throat with a profuse squirt of blood. The three squirts of blood mark a traumatic sequence. The rooster episode was traumatic for its instigator, as his nightmare about it shows. He relives it by abusing his foster brother again to even graver effect. Only he did not engineer this reliving. Nor did his victim, whose suicide in his presence shows how deeply traumatized he too was at the time even as it constitutes his own reliving in the rooster format. Who, then, was behind the videos and drawings that prompted the double reliving? Suspicion is cast on the recipient's son by a closing shot of him leaving school with the suicide's son, who has meanwhile cleared himself of suspicion. But the recipient's son was out of the traumatic loop, nor can he have intended the suicide that topped off the double reliving. It may be imagined that the sons somehow took their fathers' traumas upon themselves, the one becoming perpetrator and the other victim, but this is not

---

[16]Compounding the twofold trauma, the foster brother is an Algerian orphaned by the 1961 Paris police massacre of Algerians, itself an occluded memory. A filmic precedent of sorts for a trauma relived at someone else's instigation is Brian De Palma's *Obsession* of 1976 about a man who has traumatically lost his kidnapped wife and little girl by not paying their ransom and who relives the ordeal in some detail fifteen years later when his young bride-to-be is kidnapped—only she turns out to be his duplicitous daughter, who has secretly survived and helped stage the replay. Another precedent of sorts is *The Village* insofar as the young madcap replays the elders' traumas *en bloc*: above, p. 115.

the scenario filmed. In sum, *Caché* turns on a twofold trauma relived concurrently by the two parties to it through someone else's devising that goes unexplained.[16]

The hardest variant in my collection to swallow is Pedro Almodóvar's *Todo sobre mi madre* (*All about my mother*) of 1999. In it a son is run over before his mother's eyes on his seventeenth birthday just when she meant to tell him at long last about his paternity. His father having turned transvestite only days before she found herself pregnant by him, she had fled him precipitously by train from Barcelona to Madrid and ripped him out of her life in shock and shame. Now, seventeen years and some seven months later, that flight traumatizes her retroactively by ricochet from her son's dreadful death. She relives it a first time in reverse as, clutching the son's picture and notebook, she rides the train back from Madrid to Barcelona in search of his father. She relives it a second time, and this time once removed, through a train ride back from Barcelona to Madrid, coddling a sick baby boy lately sired on a nun by that same transvestite father and named after him like her own lost son. Finally she relives it a third time, again in reverse and again once removed, riding the rails back from Madrid to Barcelona with that baby now a healthy toddler on her lap to whom she vows never again to conceal anything out of shock or shame. Not only does this happy ending, her de-traumatization in the course of her reliving, break the reliving rules, but so in the first place does the reactivation of an old trauma by a horrendous new one which then does not itself get in on the replay, and so in the second place does the traumatization of a flight in shock and shame that is then relived with no allusion to that shock or shame. In her rush following her son's death to start reliving her flight from his father, the twice-traumatized heroine left most of her two traumas behind.

Happily, the feast of variants in James McTeigue's *V for Vendetta* of 2006 was not meant to be swallowed. Freely based on a comic strip by Alan Moore, this lot of misfire relivings unfolds behind the cover theme of an escaped internee's massive vendetta against a medical torture and killing centre serving a totalitarian British regime. Through lethal injections for the doctors who experimented on him, the escapee returns the abuse that he suffered and then some. As against traumatic reliving, this tit-for-tat-plus is deliberate, gratifying, and conclusive. Over and beyond it, that escapee from Room V (the numeral) of the official trauma mill calls himself V (the letter) and dons a mask of Guy Fawkes, who famously tried to blow up Parliament on 5 November 1606. The old refrain "Remember, remember,/The fifth of November" rings the film in as we see Fawkes caught red-handed and summarily executed. It rings the film out too as we see V caught about to blow up Parliament and summarily executed exactly four hundred years later. This anniversary recall would be mistakable for a memorial traumatic reliving were it not intentional, indeed programmatic, on V's part, his own execution inclusive. V gone, Parliament gets blown up after all by sweet Evey, V's convert rescued by him from defilement and death in police custody. Evey's parents had been brutally hauled off to bloody oblivion by those same police while Evey, then a small child, watched in mute terror from under a bed—and a shot of little Evey watching is repeated with grown Evey under a bed watching in mute terror as the same police brutally haul off the friend in whose home she is hiding out from them. As she did nothing to bring the police there, the reprise would be a mere coincidence except for V's sententious insistence that there are no coincidences. A consummate variant reliving tops off the film's run of traumas diversely recycled short of reliving proper. V had escaped his torture chamber when fire consumed the whole detention centre: twice he is shown naked in the flames, his arms raised as if in a V for victory marking his conversion to the explosive cause of freedom. His protégée Evey, although she owes him her life, remains wary of him until after he puts her through the same traumatic ordeal of torture and impending execution as he himself had endured, disguising it as a police operation against her. To round out this vicarious replay, he slips her the same pathetic messages on toilet paper as he had received from a neighbouring cell through a chink in the wall. When even in extremis she bravely refuses to betray him, he calls off the hoax: now, he tells her, she has gained true freedom as he himself had gained it. After a brief recoil, she converts to his cause heart and soul for a grand epiphany, her arms raised under a pouring rain just as his own arms had been raised amid cleansing flames. V having relived through Evey, Evey succeeds to his mantle, or mask, in the fanatical pursuit of his escalated vendetta, alias V for variant.

Variants of traumatic reliving engage movie-goers precisely as variants. What does a terrorist who puts his apprentice through his own conversion trauma have in common with a surgeon-turned-obstetrician delivering babies dead as if to save the wife he lost in childbirth? or with a French actress in Hiroshima embracing a traumatically lost wartime German lover by proxy? or with a failure to save a lamb from slaughter behind a quest to save a serial killer's intended next victim? or with a long-tormented murderess taking the blame for a killing resembling hers? or with a loving wife prostituting herself to death because her husband is sexually crippled? or with a one-man rescue squad saving surrogates galore for the uncle he inadvertently let die? or with a shattered lover recurring to the start of the ill-fated romance he meant to efface? or with two middle-aged men manipulated into recycling the one's childhood cruelty to the other? or with a wife who keeps rerunning her escape route from the husband she fled in shock? The single, overdue answer is that they each alike carry conviction only by dint of the unthinking, all-human awareness that one may go any length to relive a trauma that has been put out of mind. At the outside, one may even just imagine reliving it. Hitchcock's *Spellbound* of 1945 turns on its hero's guilty delusion of having relived his accidental killing of his kid brother in boyhood. Dino Risi's *Fantasma d'amore* (*Ghost of love*) of 1981 ups it to a mental patient twice encountering an old love only to learn each time that she is dead—and the second time, gorgeous as ever, she drowns on him to boot. As early as William Dieterle's spooky *Portrait of Jenny* of 1939 a portraitist's romance with a sitter twice ends traumatically with her drowning ten years before. Like variations on a theme in music, variations on traumatic reliving in film ring right wherever they do because they resonate with the basic, straight theme of traumatic reliving sounding through them. Their charm is double: besides each ringing right, they each ring differently.

Being visual first and last, film tends to favour such trauma and reliving as can be conveyed in starkest imagery. Even children's fare has been infiltrated. Thus in Tim Burton's *Charlie and the Chocolate Factory* of 2005 a surreal chocolate maker, long years after having been traumatically cut off by his candy-hating dentist father, names a chocolate-loving lad his heir provided he will break with his own family; in Andrew Adamson's *Chronicles of Narnia: The Lion, the Witch, and the Wardrobe* of 2005 four young siblings replay their evacuation from the Nazi air blitz on London in the magic realm of a lion king; in Christophe Gans's *Silent Hill* of 2006 an adoptive child recurs irresistibly to a world of horrors whence she issued. At the same time, brutal crime as trauma relived has become such a cinematic cliché that in his *Mystic River* of 2003 Clint Eastwood could take off from a teenage boy's abduction and abuse to make the later adult the likely suspect when he comes home blood-splattered after a local girl is murdered; even his wife has him pegged for a reverse reliving until, with traumatic irony, the splattered blood turns out to be that of a child molester he chanced to catch in the act. Conversely, few subtle inner traumas of irreparably hurt feelings find their way into film. And still fewer of the initial inner reactions to trauma known from historic and literary cases do, such as the instinctive effort to deny that a trauma is happening, or that it matters, or that it is anything new.[17] Still, for all its dearth of such finer points, my sample cinematic fare featuring traumatic reliving makes my biggest and simplest point conclusively: that the phenomenon is tacitly familiar to the movie-going public as a staple of mental life, including even to those trauma professionals who fail to recognize it professionally.

As I am no movie buff, let alone film historian, my choice of films built around traumatic reliving has been largely idiosyncratic. Whereas I could not hope for even an approximate overview of the motif in so vast a field as Western letters, I did mean to achieve one in film—and could not. To view every feature film ever released was no real option, whereas synopses in film guides rarely provide the detail needed to flag likely specimens, nor were the institutional research consultants I approached of much use.[18] So I could not correct for geographical, chronological, or other bias in the lot of films involving traumatic reliving that I did see. As these represent only an infinitesimal proportion of the feature films ever released, the absence of German, Russian, or Japanese examples from my repertory may reflect only my failure to spot any.[19] Likewise,

---

[17]Denial is, however, central to *Sous le sable*—if it counts as traumatic reliving: see above, pp. 103–104.

[18]My chief research resource was the Cinémathèque Française in Paris: to its spotty holdings and unscheduled closings it added utter incomprehension of my purpose. I approached the Cinémathèque Royale in Brussels, but its user fees proved prohibitive.

[19]Germany's traumatic defeat and revolution of 1918–1919 were continually rehashed below the surface of the German films of 1919–1929 that were most popular on the German home market, but that is something else: Monaco (1976): 115–54.

nothing would seem to account so well for my superabundance of examples from 2000 and after as that I began collecting around 2000. In any case, from the films I did draw on, I cannot see that the implicit conception of how traumatic reliving works has varied by country or by period in cinema any more than it has in Western letters since the Greeks. What may have varied in cinema by country and by period is the popularity of the motif and, to a lesser extent, the readiness of film-makers to play free and loose with it. If my sample is at all indicative, the theme appears to have been mainly French and American, to have emerged only a good third of the way through the twentieth century (perhaps only after cinematography developed sufficiently to accommodate it), to have burst into its own around 1958, and to be running wild in the present century, with variants gaining ever more on straight renditions. Only I can see no clear reasons for these indications. So, as they may be mere artifacts of my none too systematic sampling, I shall refrain from suggesting unclear reasons for them.

CHAPTER SEVEN

Reliving: Who, when, why?

What, finally, do history, literature, and film tell us about reliving trauma?

To back up to scratch yet again, the mechanism is best known from history. An individual or a group unwittingly reproduces the key pieces of a profoundly upsetting experience, or trauma, in outward disguise, often in a wholly different sphere of activity. As a rule, a traumatic experience will have struck all at once and unexpectedly. Otherwise, a prolonged traumatic ordeal that is relived will have been compacted for the purpose into a single psychological moment. Even where a traumatic impact has been piecemeal or gradual, however, as it is more usually with groups, the reliving runs to type. And as with individuals, so with groups, a traumatic reliving leaves those sufferers who survive it as if traumatized anew and hence ready to relive anew, now with two overlapping experiences to draw on. They have come full spiral.

To judge by the historic cases considered above, the most widely shared features of individual traumatic reliving are guilt felt for the trauma itself and especially a sense of acting under a higher constraint, as if on binding orders received unconsciously as in hypnosis. Individuals reliving traumas also tend to gain uncanny persuasiveness over others for the purpose while overriding any obstructive inhibitions or scruples of their own in the process. Beyond this, they may carry the relived trauma to a conclusion more drastic than the original finale even while straining in vain to fend off that dread outcome. Considered abstractly, to contrive a scenario for a reliving and then to impose it on the surrounding world may seem to argue a stronger traumatic drive than to recycle a long-dormant trauma in response to some circumstantial reminder, and yet Bismarck for one relived a seemingly superannuated personal trauma on the European stage with nightmarish intensity after taking his cue from a mere coincidence of proper names.

How closely did the relivings by historic groups that I reviewed parallel those by historic individuals? Only the Germans reliving their 1918 defeat collectively marked up a full score of features most common for individual relivings: felt guilt for the trauma and felt necessitation in reliving it; coerciveness and lawlessness on the relivers' part; a more ruinous traumatic outcome, resisted the whole joyless way. Where some features characteristic of individual reliving were inappropriate to a given collective historic case—thus Europeans reliving the Black Death, or the French Revolution run amuck, had no call to drag other continents in on the act—the collective reliving might still display those features of individual reliving that did apply. Or again, it might not. The heirs to the self-destructive frontal assault by Norman armoured horsemen at Courtrai posted no more guilt over it than did Europeans at large over the French Revolution degenerating into tyranny and terror. Nor did the politicos who jettisoned the Fourth French Republic on the precedent of the Third escalate the penalties that second time around. Where collective traumatic guilt was expiated, however, it was expiated just like individual traumatic guilt: compare the Dance of the Dead with the Berlin Bunker for damnation self-inflicted. And where collective traumatic damage was escalated, it was escalated just like individual traumatic damage, as with the French cavalry progressively from Courtrai to Crécy, Poitiers, Agincourt, and beyond.

One feature common to all the traumatic reliving in history—individual and collective alike—that I have reviewed was its felt fatality, which came of its course being known unconsciously in advance. This felt fatality was in fact the dominant feature of both kinds of reliving, individual and collective—of Lou's loves played out under a deadline as of Gonen's Jews resigned to God's will. Felt fatality is therefore arguably integral to traumatic reliving, even its defining feature, for its course is indeed preset. Yet to take individual reliving separately from collective reliving, its most striking common characteristic is rather the special powers it draws out of those afflicted. Lou's impress on history, such as it was, came of her traumatic wrestling with Nietzsche's ghost; Bismarck's was above all his *cauchemar des alliances*, Leopold's his Belgian neutrality policy, and Hitler's the Holocaust, all artifacts of traumatic reliving.[1] And to consider only collective traumas and relivings in turn, the most signal fact about those reviewed above is that they strengthen group cohesion. Gonen's Jews were never more Jewish than under persecution; the French cavalry's *esprit de corps* battened on its suicidal tactics; the Black Death created European identity from near-scratch; the failed Revolution of 1789, as relived through Romanticism and through more revolution and counter-revolution, drew Europeans closer than ever before in mind and heart around that shared culture of lost illusions on either side of the collapsible barricades; the shattering all-German trauma of 1918 led straight to the Nazi monolith. Even the Vichy trauma of 1940 and its sequel, the copycat regime change of 1958, played to an intensified national spirit despite the fratricidal political divisions that were part of the package.

The jagged parallel between ways of reliving individual and collective traumas respectively gives no hint of which kind, if either, developed first in evolutionary time. But a comparison of the individual with the collective forms of reliving is strongly suggestive. Collective reliving is more usually straight and literal, hence more primitive, which would seem to mean older. The successive replays of the disastrous cavalry offensive at Courtrai were literal all the way to World War II; they were straight too most of that way, but did finally go into simple reverse with the disastrous fixed French fortifications of the 1930s. The Black Death was replayed literally and straight as more Black Death, but also figuratively and straight as the Dance of the Dead. So was the traumatically failed French Revolution replayed across Europe literally and straight as more failed revolution, but also figuratively and straight through the Romantic

---

[1]Comparably, Janet's Irène (above, ch. 2, n. 63) relived her trauma with uncanny force while suffering from abulia otherwise.

specialty of hopes dashed, idylls foredoomed, and ideals corrupted. World War II was a straight and literal replay of World War I on the traumatized German side. By contrast, Bismarck in particular, in reliving his engagement trauma, juggled its terms beyond what any group can be imagined doing.

Traumatic reliving is common coinage in letters and movies as well as in history. This clinches its reality, lest it be thought that the mechanism discernible in history is an optical illusion. The clincher includes the variant relivings found in film, since a basic pattern must be familiar for variations on it to come across like that pattern itself. The traumas relived were all individual in the classic fiction examined as also in all but two of the films—one surrealistic, the other an individual–communal hybrid. The individual traumas relived in letters and film alike were more pinpointed and violent on the whole than were those in history. For the rest, the imaginary relivings, including the variant ones in film, showed the same common features in roughly the same proportions as did the historic relivings, with one deliberate exception that proves the rule: cinematic Grégoire Moulin feels no guilt for the trauma-bred violence he arouses all around him, his innocence being the very joke of the farce. At the same time, one or another near-typical feature of reliving was accentuated beyond range in each literary or cinematic case: witness the blind compulsion in *Ulalume*, or the deadly double guilt in *La boîte noire*. This was especially so in the filmic variants, most glaringly in the juvenile realm, what with Spider-Man's supernatural powers or V's ideologized charisma and fanaticism. Reliving itself was spotlighted and highlighted with blinding intensity in *Memento*.

Back to mere reality, where relatively few traumas get relived, however much those relivings that I singled out of history may look at home there. If the regular course of our lives is painfully broken, we can't easily get that painful break, or trauma, off our minds. But should we do so, we set ourselves up to relive it unawares—maybe. This "maybe" is too contingent for comfort. Who relives which traumas why? To ask, for starters, only who relives, might those few who do so be those incapable of producing chronic mental symptoms instead? No: Bismarck for one relived despite a prodigious neurotic output on the side. But the "who" question by itself leads nowhere in any case, for a given person or group may relive one trauma suffered and not another. So too does the "which" question by itself lead nowhere, for again and again traumas of a kind with the historic ones discussed get remembered or commemorated, affect inclusive, rather than relived. Perhaps it is those persons or groups hardest hit traumatically who relive? Again a no from Bismarck, whose blow from the courtship and gambling fiasco that he relived hardly begins to match the impact of countless unrelived traumas that haunt our refugee camps, emergency shelters, or military wards. Perhaps, then, relivers relive not their severest traumas, but those for which they feel guiltiest? Be it remembered here that guilt felt for traumas is disproportionate to real guilt for them; otherwise Europeans would never have relived the Black Death or, outside of France, the failed French Revolution. Besides, a trauma that one is truly guilty of having brought upon oneself is that much harder to stop remembering along with the affect that it aroused. Degrees of felt guilt are accordingly as irrelevant as degrees of felt pain to who relives which traumas, let alone why.

What, then, is relevant? Our first biographic case considered, that of Lou Andreas-Salomé, suggests that one precondition for reliving a trauma might be the successful denial of the key traumatic element. He did not reject me: such was the message implicit in Lou's Nietzsche book and explicit in her tale "Geschwister", Nietzsche having in reality dumped her with a traumatic thud. To the same effect, Germany defeated in 1918 notoriously denied the fact, as when Friedrich Ebert, the political heir to this defeat as first postwar German chancellor, told the German troops returning from the front: "No enemy vanquished you." So far, so good—but now objections crowd in concerning other traumas relived. Did plagued Europe deny the pestilence, or the Romantics deny that the Revolution had led to the Terror? Did Bismarck deny his broken engagement, or Leopold his queen's death at his hands? These objections can perhaps be met at least partway. Take just Europe after the Black Death: a case can be made from chroniclers' accounts, or from booming birth rates, or from Boccaccio's bawdy survivors' tales, that if Europeans did not quite deny the pandemic, they moved from it with shrug-like alacrity. But the capacity to gloss over or dismiss unpleasant realities to the point of denial is well-nigh universal even if Lou did have more than her fair share of it. Therefore as a requirement for reliving traumas it would say next to nothing about who relives which traumas why.

The irrelevance of felt guilt or felt pain to the whys and wherefores of traumatic reliving is most obvious from the fact that, in reality no less than in legend, one may relive a trauma not one's own. Or actually the single such historic reliving that I have studied in depth was of a trauma that even for its original victim was traumatic only on a poetic licence, like Francesca's death in Dante's vision. The Bavarian monarch Ludwig II, committed for insanity on 11 June 1886, drowned mysteriously with his psychiatric guardian in shallow water two days later. In January 1889, with true traumatic illogic, his younger kinsman Crown Prince Rudolf of Habsburg, fearing "an 11 June" for himself in turn, re-staged this very event that he feared: he contrived a double death for himself at Mayerling that matched Ludwig's point for point, distortedly yet unmistakably, as if in a bad dream about it.[2] Ludwig's fate, being tragic, had aroused Rudolf's pity and terror. What Rudolf re-enacted was not, however, his traumatic experience of Ludwig's fate in pity and terror; rather, he re-enacted that tragic fate itself with himself in Ludwig's place.[3] In all the fictive cases I know of reliving others' traumas, from ancient myth to modern movies, the traumas relived have likewise been those of older blood relatives, suggesting a mysterious trauma-bearing blood link.[4] Reliving one's own traumas is trouble enough to fathom. Reliving others' traumas adds such confusion that I would gladly deny the evidence for it if I could. Failing that, I can only venture that the reliving mechanism enjoys enough autonomy in mental life to kick

---

[2]Binion (1975).

[3]Compare Janet's Irène, who replayed her mother's part in her trauma along with her own: above, ch. 2, n. 13.

[4]Cf. above, pp. 4–5, on the Greek theogony and Grillparzer's "tragedy of fate", and Binion (1997): 33–44, on the Tristan legend. In Georges Lacombe's 1945 film *Le pays sans étoiles* (*The country without stars*), adapted from a novel of that name by Pierre Véry, a youngster falls in love with the same young woman as did a predecessor in his blood line a century before, and he jumps off the same cliff after murdering an equivalent rival (best friend in lieu of brother). *Caché* may belong in this cinematic company: above, pp. 120–21. The movie *V for Vendetta* would be an exception to the blood link if V can be seen as reliving Guy Fawkes's trauma: above, pp. 121–22. Back to reality, Rudolf may have relived Ludwig's trauma the more readily in that royal personages have been mimicking other royal personages at least since the Roman emperor Hadrian saw himself as Pericles, Augustus, and other earlier notables by turns: Birley (1997): 2, 111, 201, 218–19, 296, 306, and passim.

in without rhyme or reason anywhere that trauma has struck. As for a given trauma being replicated within a family by mere happenstance, I beg off altogether.[5]

What about the "why" of traumatic reliving? Reliving traumas does not serve to prevent painful remembering, for the reliving mechanism kicks in only where the painful remembering has already been blocked. Thereafter the mechanism repeats, and often augments, the initial traumatic pain to no apparent benefit. Its frequent overlap with retaliation suggests a master need behind both to return harm for harm, pain for pain. Unlike retaliation, however, reliving may punish a substitute traumatic offender, or even the self as arch culprit. Again unlike retaliation, reliving doesn't resolve the need behind it, the way scratching doesn't stop itching, so that the overlap with retaliation, which does usually bring closure, looks merely fortuitous. Might the mechanism, which promotes group cohesion, have emerged among groups for that purpose in days of yore? Hardly, as ritualized remembrance serves that purpose at less cost. Nor did the classic fictionists have any one answer. The "why" of reliving was fate for Euripides and for Racine, guilt for Dante, and deep compulsion for Poe, Melville, and Ibsen—so many prominent features of reliving in the historic record, but no explanation for it. The movie-makers, finally, while hoisting the compulsion to relive sky-high, leave the "why" of it out of account. And indeed, that "why" of traumatic reliving is no more necessarily the fictionists' or movie-makers' business than is the "why" of human love or greed or prankishness, or of whatever else fictionists or movie-makers may deal in. In sum, they have merely helped to lay out the problem for us to solve.

Having reached a dead end in the quest for the who, which, and why of traumatic reliving, let us try next whether the how of it leads farther forward—after the brief backtracking that such a try requires.

---

[5]Pedro Almodóvar filmed such a family curse in *Volver (Turnabout)* of 2006. There a woman has murdered her husband after he raped one of their daughters, producing a girl; the raped daughter's later husband has legitimated the girl and attempts to rape her in turn; the girl kills him in fighting him off, whereupon her mother takes the deed upon herself without knowing that her own mother had murdered her own rapist father any more than her daughter knows who begat her how.

There is no reliving a trauma knowingly, for a reliving must preserve a preponderant conscious uncertainty as to its outcome in order for it to be traumatic in its turn. Ordinarily a trauma is not relived but instead keeps being remembered in all its pain, in which case it hurts less and less with time, like a bruise that heals. Sometimes, however, the traumatic affect, be it shame, disgust, fear, anguish, humiliation, or whatever, may be denied early along by an act of will. Then it does not vanish or even diminish; rather, it survives intact on hold. Such denial of the traumatic affect is a precondition for reliving a trauma. In other words, those who relive a trauma have ostensibly put its devastating impact behind them while in fact only setting the feel of that impact aside. But reliving does not automatically follow on such denial—far from it. Most commonly a denied affect will erupt in unguarded moments as an outburst of anger, say, or a burst of tears, and then we say quite rightly that the afflicted party had been "holding it in".[6] Or else the denied affect can go on being denied indefinitely without the trauma ever being relived. A reliving, if one does come to pass, undoes the denial halfway in that it rejoins the pain to the trauma vicariously—that is, it rejoins the pain to a re-edition of the trauma that fronts for it in consciousness. The pain thus recurs like a nudge out of the depths with the message: Here is the feeling that you have been denying. And in those depths, as the reliving builds up to its climax, it is fully expected to reopen the old wound, yet it goes forward all the same. In this it is like an unconscious self-punishment with the dénouement inscribed: You've got this coming. This inscription befits the guilt for the trauma that the sufferer mostly tends to feel regardless of any real liability for it. The pressure from the denied affect to reassert itself, to rejoin the trauma being relived, reinforces the sense of inevitability or fatedness that accompanies the reliving on its headlong push to its foregone conclusion. Seen in this perspective, who relives under the suggestive effect of circumstances and who coerces circumstances in order to relive would seem to depend respectively on the stronger or weaker denial of the traumatic affect. Thus Bismarck appears to have convinced himself that Isabella Loraine was good riddance where Hitler could not quite convince himself that his

---

[6]More clinically, episodic hypertension has been traced to traumatic anxiety relived unconsciously: Mann (1998).

mother's terminal suffering was inevitable.[7] But even this much, or little, about whether or not a trauma gets relived can be known only inferentially if at all—a meager net yield of our switch from analyzing the who, which, and why to the how of reliving trauma.

Do the works of literary fiction reviewed square with this rudimentary inside account of trauma relived? Only incompletely, in that they all focus on the reliving proper, with the back story and the crucial build-up to the reliving supplied only by recalls. Even so, the congruence is striking as far as it goes. Euripides's Creusa has, princess-like, put her rape by Apollo and ensuing child exposure firmly enough behind her that it takes a chance encounter many years later with that child himself, albeit consciously unrecognized, to prompt her reliving. She had meanwhile kept her traumatic remorse in abeyance by somatizing it—by converting it into sterility. Only when she goes to Apollo's own shrine to inquire its cause does its connection with Apollo himself begin to dawn on her, reopening the old wound and launching the reliving. In the end that reliving is thwarted, however, as Ion escapes her death plot, mother and child recognize each other, the traumatic spell lifts, and the traumatic affect dissolves, cutting short our comparison with historic reliving. In Dante's time frame of timelessness, Francesca's reliving has begun surreally with her trauma itself: her murder in the act of lust with Paolo. She denies the trauma in effect in that she deletes both the lust and the murder from her truncated self-presentation, which she confines to her first fateful moment of tenderness with Paolo. She does, though, vent her traumatic rage and outrage during one of her brief periodic respites as over and over the two ex-bodies mime their act of lust cut short. Thus the traumatic affect has rejoined the trauma being relived. For Racine's Athalia the traumatic affect is a mix of horror and remorse over having slain her grandson following her mother's ghastly murder. She puts that affect behind her royal decorum as best she can, but then it resurfaces in a nightmare recall of the trauma and preview of her reliving it in

[7]Thus too Janet's Irène, whose relivings were triggered circumstantially in the main (above, ch. 2, n. 63). Only after she had brought the pathogenic trauma to full conscious memory (through six months' hypnotic treatment) could Irène begin to restore the affect to it. In the literature discussed, Creusa needs a trigger to relive, having put her traumatic affects on hold, while for the opposite reason Ahab and Rosmer do not.

horror and remorse combined. The poet-narrator of Poe's *Ulalume* has detached the traumatic affect of ghastly gloom from his traumatic memory of having buried his lost love. Eerily, the affect comes back over him without the corresponding memory and guides his steps back to her crypt before he knows it. Melville's Ahab, although obsessively mindful of the material facts of his encounter with Moby Dick, denies his traumatic humiliation by the beast to the point of denying his mutilation itself in his heart of hearts: in the deadly throes of reliving he accounts his whale-bone leg as much himself as any other bone in his body. Finally, Ibsen's Rosmer remains mired in the traumatic horror of his wife's suicide without quite seeing why: that he had wanted her dead. To that extent even he, who relives consciously against all the rules, has detached the traumatic affect from its traumatic cause. On this reality test for classic fiction, the aggregate score is a high pass.

In contrast to literary works, movies tend to privilege the mere surface of traumatic reliving if only because movies meet the eye first and foremost. They nonetheless corroborate the historic indications to the modest extent that they show trauma victims hiding their traumatic pain behind hard-boiled cynicism, or professional decorum, or patrician dignity, or public posturing, or the simple need to survive, as a precondition for reliving a die-hard trauma. Of my cinematic specimens, *Memento* alone probes the mental phenomenon down in its depths—too far down indeed, for what it displays is the unconscious experience of reliving and not its interplay with consciousness, consciousness being foreshortened in traumatized Leonard's case for that very purpose by a figurative blow to the head.

What about the subjective experience of reliving by traumatized groups? A rough equivalence with traumatized individuals may be surmised by analogy and finds some support in outer signs of mass mood. For the rest, however, we cannot advance securely beyond conjecture. Whereas we may empathize with historic individuals given the requisite information and concentration, the inner experience of groups as such is inaccessible to us in our present conceptual poverty. Outwardly seen, a group that relives a trauma is a fluid mass of individuals acting in concert for reasons more or less foreign to them as individuals. But that group has no locus of subjacent emotivity or memory in any known brain cells of its members or in any occult collective recess. Rather, the group effect derives, not from its members' bodies lumped together, but from their interaction, with no discernible physical localization for it. There is no coping with groups on such intangible terms, but neither is there any coping with traumatic reliving if groups are discounted. And there, at this impasse, our analysis must pause.

I have left no stones unturned that I can see in this quest to understand traumatic reliving. Where, then, do all these advances and retreats of our enquiry leave us? They leave us with a syndrome of unknown origin that is universally familiar and can be characterized with some precision, but that comes into play or doesn't as if arbitrarily, or at all odds according to countless elusive unpredictables. A typical candidate for reliving a trauma could not be profiled. A trauma more apt than another to be relived could not be delineated. No reasons good or bad could be found for reliving a trauma instead of remembering it in all its painfulness. Finally, the inner experience of traumatic reliving could be reconstructed only for individuals as against groups. This bizarre phenomenon of traumatic reliving thus runs like a wild card through history with momentous impact on public and private life. Nor is order within chaos to be sought in some subtle regularity beyond steady traumatic recall on the one side or serial traumatic reliving on the other, for the issue is the whys and wherefores of serial reliving and not some potential pattern of occurrence and recurrence. In matters psychohistorical, as in so much else, the orderly universe dear to science just isn't with us, at least not today. Maybe tomorrow.

REFERENCES

Andreas-Salomé, L. (1885). *Im Kampf um Gott*. Leipzig: W. Friedrich.

Andreas-Salomé, L. (1921). Geschwister. *Deutsche Rundschau, 19 October 1921*: 24–63.

Assemblée Nationale. (1947). *Rapport fait au nom de la commission chargée d'enquêter sur les événements survenus en France de 1933 à 1945*. Paris: Imprimerie de l'Assemblée Nationale and Presses Universitaires de France.

Balzac, H.d. (1832–1844). *Le colonel Chabert*, ed. Pierre Citron. Paris: Marcel Didier [reprinted 1961].

Balzac, H.d. (1834–1850). Adieu. *La comédie humaine, 10*: 973–1014. Paris: Gallimard [reprinted 1979].

Binion, R. (1968). *Frau Lou/: Nietzsche's Wayward Disciple*. Princeton, NJ: Princeton University Press.

Binion, R. (1975). From Mayerling To Sarajevo. *Journal of Modern History, 47*: 280–316.

Binion, R. (1976). *Hitler among the Germans*. New York: Elsevier.

Binion, R. (1981a). Repeat performance. Leopold III and Belgian neutrality. In: *Soundings Psychohistorical and Psycholiterary* (pp. 15–61). New York: Psychohistory Press.

Binion, R. (1981b). The play as replay or the key to Pirandello's *Six Characters in Search of an Author, Henry IV*, and *Clothe the Naked*. In: *Soundings Psychohistorical and Psycholiterary* (pp. 127–153). New York: Psychohistory Press.

Binion, R. (1986). *After Christianity: Christian Survivals in Post-Christian Culture*. Durango, CO: Logbridge-Rhodes.

Binion, R. (1990). Romanticism and the revolution of 1789. In: Robert Aldrich (Ed.), *France: Politics, Society, Culture and International Relations. Papers from the Seventh George Rudé Seminar in French History and Civilisation, The University of Sydney, 21–23 July 1990* (pp. 115–130). Sydney: Department of Economic History, University of Sydney.

Binion, R. (1993). *Love Beyond Death: The Anatomy of a Myth in the Arts*. New York: New York University Press.

Binion, R. (1994a). Vom Sterben betrunken: Sigmund Freud als Kulturerscheinung seiner Zeit. *Inn, 11*: 17–23.

Binion, R. (1994b). Ketzerisches zur Kriegsfrage. *"So ist der Mensch ..." 80 Jahre Erster Weltkrieg*: 117–124. Vienna: Museen der Stadt Wien.

Binion, R. (1995). *Freud über Krieg und Aggression: einerlei oder zweierlei?* Vienna: Picus.

Binion, R. (1997). *Sounding the Classics: From Sophocles to Thomas Mann*. Westport, CT: Greenwood/Praeger.

Binion, R. (2003a). Traumatic Reliving in History. *Annual of Psychoanalysis, 31*: 237–250.

Binion, R. (2003b). Bush's America goes to war. *Clio's Psyche, 10*: 1–3.

Binion, R. (2004). Europe's Culture of Death. In: Jerry, S. Piven (Ed.), *The Psychology of Death in Fantasy and History* (pp. 119–135). Westport, CT: Praeger.

Binion, R. (2005a). Bismarck's alliance nightmare. *Clio's Psyche, 12*: 25–26.

Binion, R. (2005b). *Past Impersonal: Group Process in Human History*. DeKalb, IL: Northern Illinois University Press.

Binion, R. (2005c). De Gaulle as Pétain. *Clio's Psyche, 12*: 37, 56–66, 97–100.

Birley, A. (1997). *Hadrian: The Restless Emperor*. London: Routledge.

Bismarck, O. (1934). *Die gesammelten Werke* [The Collected Works], *15*. Berlin: Stollberg.

Byron, G. (1922). *Correspondence, 2*, ed. John Murray. London: John Murray.

Carlson, M. (1974). Patterns of structure and character in Ibsen's *Rosmersholm*. *Modern Drama, 17*: 267–275.

Caruth, C. (1996) *Unclaimed Experience: trauma, narrative, and history*. Baltimore: Johns Hopkins University Press.

Chu, J.A. (1998). The Repetition Compulsion Revisited: Reliving Dissociated Trauma. *Psychotherapy, 28(2)*: 327–332.

Cronacher, D.J. (1967). *Euripidean Drama: Myth, Theme and Structure.* Toronto: University of Toronto Press.

Dick, P. (1974). A little something for us tempunauts. *Final Stage.* New York: Ballantine.

Domarus, M. (1965). *Hitler: Reden und Proklamationen.* Munich: Süddeutscher Verlag.

Duras, M. (1960). *Hiroshima mon amour: scénario et dialogues.* Paris: Gallimard.

Engelberg, E. (1985). *Bismarck. Urpreusse und Reichsgründer.* Berlin: Siedler.

Esterson, A. (1998). Jeffrey Masson and Freud's seduction theory: A new fable based on old myths. *History of the Human Sciences, 11*: 1–21.

Euripides (c. 410 B.C.). Ion. In: *The Bacchae and Other Plays.* Trans. Philip Vellacott (pp. 35–82). Hammondsworth: Penguin [reprinted 1954].

Euripides (406 B.C.). *The Bacchae.* Trans. C.K. Williams. New York: Farrar, Straus and Giroux [reprinted 1990].

Fish, S. (1989). *Doing What Comes Naturally: Change, Rhetoric, and the Practice of Theory in Literary and Legal Studies.* Durham, NC: Duke University Press.

Freud, S. (1940–1968). *Gesammelte Werke chronologisch geordnet* [Collected Works in Chronological Order]. 18 vols. London: Imago.

Freud, S. (1986). *Briefe an Wilhelm Fliess 1887–1904* [Letters to Wilhelm Fliess 1887–1904]. Frankfurt: Fischer.

Garçon, M. (Ed.) (1946). *Le procès Laval. Compte rendu sténographique.* Paris: Albin Michel.

Gaulle, C.d. (1941). *Discours et messages du général de Gaulle, Première Série, 18 juin 1940–8 octobre 1941.* Cairo: Éditions "France Toujours".

Giannopoulou, V. (2000). Divine agency and tyche in Euripides' *Ion*: Ambiguity and shifting perspectives. In: C. Martin, L. Kevin & S. David (Eds.), *Euripides and Tragic Theatre in the Late Fifth Century* (pp. 257–271). Champaign, IL: Stripes.

Gonen, J.Y. (1975). *A Psychohistory of Zionism.* New York: Mason/Charter.

Gonen, J.Y. (1979). The Israeli illusion of omnipotence following the Six Days War. *Journal of Psychohistory, 6*: 241–271.

Gonen, J.Y. (2005). *Yahweh versus Yahweh: The Enigma of Jewish History.* Madison, WI: University of Wisconsin Press.

Graziano, F. (2004). *Wounds of Love: The Mystic Marriage of Saint Rose of Lima.* New York: Oxford University Press.

Hemingway, E. (1926). *The Sun Also Rises.* New York: Scribner [reprinted 2003].

Huys, M. (1995). *The Tale of the Hero Who Was Exposed at Birth in Euripidean Tragedy: A Study of Motifs.* Leuven: Leuven University Press.

Ibsen, Henrik. (1886). Rosmersholm. *Nutidsdramaer 1877–99*: 279–327. Oslo: Gyldendal [reprinted 1992].

Jackson, J. (2003). *The Fall of France: The Nazi Invasion of 1940*. Oxford: Oxford University Press.

Jäckel, E. (1958). Charles de Gaulle und die Vierte Französische Republik. *Geschichte in Wissenschaft und Unterricht, 9*: 490–504.

Janet, P. (1911). *L'État mental des hystériques* [The mental state of hysterics], 2nd ed. Paris: Alcan.

Janet, P. (1919). *Les médications psychologiques* [Psychological medications]. 2. Paris: Alcan.

Janet, P. (1920). *The Major Symptoms of Hysteria*. New York: Macmillan.

Janet, P. (1928). *L'évolution de la mémoire et de la notion du temps* [The Evolution of Memory and of the Time Sense]. Paris: Chanine.

Künstlicher, R. (1998). Horror at pleasure of his own of which he himself is not aware: The case of the rat man. In: I. Matthis & I. Szecsödy (Eds.), *On Freud's Couch: Seven New Interpretations of Freud's Case Histories* (pp. 127–162). Northvale, NJ: Jason Aronson.

Lacouture, J. (1984). *De Gaulle, I, Le rebelle*. Paris: Seuil.

Levy, M.S. (2000). A Conceptualization of the Repetition Compulsion. *Psychiatry, 63*: 45–53.

Mann, S.J. (1998). *Healing Hypertension: A Revolutionary New Approach*. New York: Wiley.

Markowitz, J. (1969). *The Psychodynamic Evolution of Groups*. New York: Vantage.

Melville, H. (1851). *Moby-Dick* or *The Whale*. Evanston, IL: Northwestern University Press and The Newbury Library [reprinted 1988].

Monaco, P. (1976). *Cinema & Society: France and Germany During the Twenties*. New York: Elsevier.

Nietzsche, F. (1887). *Die fröhliche Wissenschaft* [The Gay Science]. Leipzig: E.W. Fritzsch.

Noguères, L. (1955). *Le véritable procès du Maréchal Pétain*. Paris: Fayard.

Orlandini, A. (2004). Repetition compulsion in a trauma victim: Is the "analgesia principle" beyond the pleasure principle? Clinical implications. *Journal of the American Academy of Psychoanalysis and Dynamic Psychiatry, 32*: 525–540.

Palmer, A. (1976). *Bismarck*. London: Wiedenfeld and Nicolson.

Paxton, R.O. (1972). *Vichy France: Old Guard and New Order, 1940–1944*. New York: Knopf.

Pflanze, O. (1990). *Bismarck and the Development of Germany*, 1. Princeton, NJ: Princeton University Press.

Pirandello, L. (1922). Enrico IV [Henry IV]. *Maschere nude* [Naked Masks]. Verona: Mondadori [reprinted 1947].

Poe, E.A. (1848). Ulalume. In: Thomas Ollive Mabbott (Ed.), *Edgar Allan Poe: Complete Poems* (pp. 409–423). Urbana, IL: University of Illinois Press [reprinted 1969].

Proust, M. (1913–1927). *À la recherche du temps perdu* [Remembrance of Things Past]. Paris: NRF.

Racine, J. (1690). *Oeuvres complètes*, ed. Raymond Picard. Paris: Gallimard [reprinted 1950].

Rémond, R. (1987). *Le retour de de Gaulle*. Brussels: Complexe.

République Française, Haute Cour de Justice. (1945). *Procès du Maréchal Pétain: Compte rendu in extenso des audiences*. Paris: Imprimerie des Journaux Officiels.

République Française, Assemblée Nationale. (1958). *Débats parlementaires*. Paris: Imprimerie des Journaux Officiels.

Rousso, H. (1987). *Le syndrome de Vichy de 1944 à nos jours*. Paris: Seuil.

Shapiro, B. (2009). *Traumatic Politics: The Deputies and the King in the Early French Revolution*. University Park, PA: Pennsylvania State University Press.

Sterne, L. (1767). *Tristram Shandy*. New York: Knopf [reprinted 1929].

Szaluta, J. (1980). Apotheosis to ignominy: The martyrdom of Marshal Pétain. *Journal of Psychohistory, 7*: 415–454.

Szecsödy, I. (1998). Dora: Freud's Pygmalion or the unrecovered patient of a famous analyst? In: I. Matthis and I. Szecsödy (Eds.), *On Freud's Couch: Seven New Interpretations of Freud's Case Histories* (pp. 57–92). Northvale, NJ: Jason Aronson.

Terr, L. (1990). *Too Scared To Cry: Psychic Trauma In Childhood*. New York: Harper & Row.

Van der Kolk, B.A. (1987). *Psychological trauma*. Washington, DC: American Psychiatric Press.

Van der Kolk, B.A. (1989). The compulsion to repeat the trauma: Re-enactment, revictimization and masochism. *The Psychiatric Clinics of North America, 12(2)*: 389–411.

Winock, M. (1968). *La fièvre hexagonale: Les grandes crises politiques de 1871 à 1968*. Paris: Calmann-Lévy.

Winock, M. (1978). *La république se meurt: Chronique 1956–1958*. Paris: Seuil.

INDEX